# GOD
## *The* HERE
## *and the*
# HEREAFTER

### NORMAN B. TALSOE

**GOD - The HERE and the HEREAFTER**
Copyright © 2022 by Norman B. Talsoe

ISBN:     Paperback:     979-8986428307
          Hardback:      979-8986428314
          eBook:         979-8986428321

Printed in the United States of America

**Norman Talsoe Publishing**

# TABLE OF CONTENTS

**Craig Talsoe,** *I believe this to be an eye-opening read for all believers and believers in Christ. My father put many years into researching this book. His dream told him that he would believe the task to be impossible. Moreover, this effort has helped me understand questions I had in the Bible. I hope all in all that you find the book informative and enjoyable.*

**Connie Tropple (Talsoe)** *I highly recommend this book to anyone, no matter how secure you feel in your faith. It gives insight into Biblical information most people have not even considered. Just believing in God is not enough!--this book covers what is needed and has changed how I want to live out the rest of my time.*

**Cara Belisle (Talsoe)** *This book aims to evangelize the world. It explains the chronological order of events happening in the book of Revelations. For believers and unbelievers, this book brings a message of hope through understanding what we need to do in preparing for the return of Christ, our Lord and Saviour. After reading this book, I have come to a more profound love, a better understanding, and a stronger faith in Jesus Christ and what He has prepared for us in the Hereafter. The rewards make it worth sharing this book with family and friends to help spread God's word. God bless.*

# PREFACE

Are you interested in reading about mysteries involving you without your knowledge? The thing is, we are all involved in the story I am about to tell. So, depending on who you are, you will believe me or say, "you are out of your mind."

I was eighty-two-year-old when I started writing a book God asked me to write. I am now ninety-one: hardly the age to be an author. So why am I doing this? The LORD used multiple miracles in every step of convincing me to honor His request; *how do you say no to God?* Whether Christian or Atheist, the impossible sequence of events could not be due to random chance: but to God. The task involves interpreting the Biblical last seven years of God's 6000-year week. While sounding insanely impossible: the following story is all true. God will determine the consequences of your reaction.

# THE VISION

Before waking one morning, I received a realistic vision asking me to write a book with the given title: *"God," the "Here," and the "Hereafter."* The image appeared in black, "Old English," italic print on a pure white background. An accompanying information burst said; that **the book would help evangelize the world** *in the end-times.* I immediately thought **this came from the LORD or, in retrospect, from my head**. It was totally out of character. All the information flashed at once. While in the vision, I said: ***"You've got to be kidding – why me -- this is impossible. How can I possibly do this?"***

This dream happened to me early in 2012, preceded by a previous one in 2010. It similarly delivered a ***"Time is short"*** message, alluding to the imminent return of Christ. However, this vision was in dark black letters on a bright blood-red background. I had to believe these combined visions came from the Almighty and immediately labeled them *"**My Impossible Dream**."* How could I respond to such a request? Nevertheless, my *impossible* dream impression became a particular link that, coupled with future events, drove me to write this book.

Next, God sent me a sign that my previous supernatural event was not from me. The following Sunday, in a sermon titled ***"Would you like to change the World"*** by Geoff Bohleen, the Family Ministries Pastor for Wooddale Church. A quote, *in the discourse*, from:

> (Matthew 28:18-20) [18] And Jesus spoke to them, saying, "All authority has been given to Me in heaven and on earth. [19] Go therefore and make disciples of all the nations, baptizing them in the name of the Father and of the Son and the Holy Spirit, [20] teaching them to observe all things that I have commanded you; and lo, I am with you always, even to the end of the age." Amen.

He followed the sermon by preaching, "He told them to change the world!" and "change the world was through making disciples of people in all the nations." And "There is no question that we are to be engaged in evangelism. `The question is, "What approaches are we to take as we tell others about Jesus?" The **_sermon was about evangelizing the world_**. It was directed at me and prompted me to ask the pastor for a copy. Numerous statements and scriptures from that address played the same theme and reinforced the information I had received in my dream., Geoff delivered a message that validated my vision:: it now became more believable. I prayed to God for more proof that my dream was not mine. But instead, the most solid reinforcement came from a different source. Within the past few years, I had heard and became a big follower of then 10-year-old singer Jackie Evancho.

In describing this little girl's performance, I had always said; that it was like watching a miracle happen. She would change from a giggly little girl to this angelic performer and back to a typical 10-year-old. All this while being incredibly humble. When asked where she got her talent, she would shyly say, "From God." When further questioned how she prepared for the performance, she said: "I do a penguin waddle to relax and give a short prayer asking God to sing with me." She had taken the world by storm by placing second in "America's Got Talent." Being a huge fan, I transcribed one of her songs from a video that would allow me to hear only her voice. _Mysteriously tacked onto the end of her song was a male voice quoting (Matthew 13:44-52) the parable of the "buried treasure," "the pearl," and the "Dragnet." The buried treasure and the pearl were metaphors for the Kingdom of Heaven._ I had transcribed the song two years earlier, in 2010, before He requested me to write His book. **_I had not paid attention to the title_** -- at that time, there was no significance, having transcribed it six months before my latest dream. That addition told me two years before the book writing invitation; its narrative was to instruct everyone **on how** to become heaven ready to satisfy God's expectations.

Nevertheless, these ending parables made me extremely curious: they should not have been there. They were just, what appeared to be, an awkward part of the montage, something that did not seem to belong. That the parables were part of this song makes it so astonishing.

So what was the song title that I transcribed with the attached parables? In a serendipitous moment, it all came together. That moment occurred when **_the song's title_**, **_"The Impossible Dream," with its parables,_** matched my description of His **_Impossible_** task.

Then it sunk in -- linking it to my self-described "**_Impossible Dream,_**" a sledgehammer finally hit home. God had validated my perception of this impossible task and further, with the attached parables, described what He wanted the book to emphasize. I.e., _humanity's ultimate goal should be the Kingdom of Heaven._

In that fist-to-forehead moment, **_I lost it; tears fell as I realized, for the first time, that this dream came from the Almighty._** _For unfathomable reasons, I became convinced that God had selected me to do this impossible task of delivering His message._ As if that was not enough, the sermon preached the following Sunday was on the **same parables**. Of the "buried treasure," "the pearl," and the "Dragnet" attached to the "The Impossible Dream" sung by Jackie with, believably, God, as she prayerfully requested, accompanying. I became hooked.

# ACKNOWLEDGMENTS

As I approached this impossible task, the first support came from my cousin Wayne and his wife, Deedy Harmala. They are both dedicated Christians and were the first I dared talk to about what happened to me. It took me three months before I even had the nerve to speak to them, -- and I know them well – how could I ever tell anyone that God had asked me to write a book while giving me the title – and then say it would help evangelize the world in the end-times?

From strangers or unbelievers, I envisioned "rolled eyeballs" and a sympathetic head nod with a look of pity. Nevertheless, I knew I would get a sympathetic ear from my cousin and his wife. As a result, we have had many excellent discussions concerning religion, atheism, Christianity, and what I have been writing. They were among the first to read my offering and give suggestions. Then there were my children Connie, Cara, and Craig, who read my book as it evolved, and they and their spouses became regular church-going Christians in the process. Others from Wooddale Church would include Tom Correll, a CDC colleague, and retired Missions pastor who reviewed my writings and gave valuable advice, Gary Puffett, Pat Mazarol, and Pastor Geoff Bohlen. Geoff delivered a sermon on evangelizing the world linked to my dream, and Pastor Shawn Winters preached on the three parables attached to the song related to my vision a week later. My good and close friend Dan O'Connor – a very faithful Christian, was always available for discussions in Colorado. I must also thank David Aeilts from Wooddale for advice on structuring my book and Joel and Kay Critzer from Bible Study for reviewing early versions. When I got up the nerve to mention what I was doing to my friends, ex-roommates when we were single, Buz Anderson, Duane Schley with Carl Johnson, my ex-Univac boss, who joined the group, I did not even get a single eye roll. They became valuable sounding boards over the years, as I wrote.

Of course, I dare not forget to mention my secretary, Carol, from Univac, 50 plus years ago; she, early on, sent me a link of Jackie Evancho singing "To Believe." In becoming an instant fan, I sought her songs, which were not on her CDs or DVDs, resulting in the transcription of a video _that convinced me to write this book_. The song was "The Impossible Dream" and had the three parables attached to the end. I continue to play her songs every day.

# INTRODUCTION

Most everyone knows enough about God, His Son Jesus, His birth, crucifixion, and He will return. However, many do not know that we are closer to Jesus's return than they think.; it will be in your children's lifetime, if not yours. This book will help educate believers who think they know the way to Salvation: but do not. It will also offer nonbelievers the opportunity to change their minds. The narrative will cover the last seven years of tribulation until Christ returns. One cannot help but see the increased vitriol between people and political parties that resonates with Matthew 24: scripture foretelling these things is in the Bible. [7] For nation will rise against nation and kingdom against kingdom. And there will be famines, pestilences, and earthquakes in various places.

> [9]"Then they will deliver you up to tribulation and kill you, and you will be hated by all nations for My name's sake. [10] And then many will be offended, will betray one another, and will hate one another. [11] Then many false prophets will rise and deceive many."

The journey through the book of Revelation will end with Christ winning against Satan. However, the ravages of war leading to the final battle will wipe out more than 50% of the earth's evil population. Therefore, everyone who wants to survive must be acceptable to Jesus. Find out what that means. We are approaching the end of God's week, defined in Scripture as one day equals one thousand years. i.e., meaning His week is 6000 years. The proof is available with a bit of research.

| | |
|---|---|
| Adam to Noah | 1656 years |
| Noah to Christ | 2340 years |
| Christ to now | <u>2022</u> years |
| | 6017 years |

God's week is at its end. Forecasted prophecies of what is to come are horrendous. Today's stressful existence closely matches Matthew24's prediction for us. A thoughtful person would want to know if they should be concerned with what they intuitively know is coming. Why else would God have me write this book if it was not to warn you?

# COINCIDENCES

"Coincidence is God's way of remaining anonymous" Albert Einstein, The World As I See It. However, unbelievers often cite; it's random to explain what happened no matter how improbable the event.

If one rolled two dice to be a seven consecutively a thousand times, would that be random _or of God_? Intuitively, we would know it was from God if we saw that. Comparably, a _random dice roll_ would get three consecutive sixes out of one hundred rolls.

Coincidences are what we often say; "It was meant to be" – things that happen and significantly influence our lives, but we have no clue why they occur. The above quote from Einstein refers to God in a cosmic sense rather than a personal God. It is fascinating how Einstein, an unbeliever of formal religions, became a deist - a believer in an impersonal creator God, a "Cosmic God."

Some speculate that because Einstein agreed to recognize that the universe had a beginning, it demanded some form of God. A deist believes in the existence of a creator who does not intervene in the universe. His beliefs were based strictly on earth-bound reasoning that refuses to believe in the supernatural, i.e., a personal God interacting with humanity. For many believers, "There are no accidents in God's universe -- or our lives." Many odd things occur to us all, leaving the question: "Why did that just happen?" Terms like SYNCHRONICITY start entering into our vocabulary. Synchronicity happens when two or more events, which are causally unrelated, rather than related, occur meaningfully. In being synchronous, the actions should be unlikely to happen together by chance, but against all the odds, they still do. Many believe there are numerous universal laws or truths in God's universe that one can never positively prove; "coincidence" is one.

# GOD

(Matthew 22:35-40) "You shall love the Lord your God with all your heart, with all your soul, and with all your mind, and You shall love your neighbor as yourself."

## Atheist Beliefs

One atheist community argues that a loving and benevolent God would not sentence anyone to existence in an eternal lake of fire, claiming cruel and unusual punishment. As an example, Charles Darwin wrote In his autobiography answering the question:

***Will a Loving God Punish People Forever in Hades? "Thus disbelief crept over me at a very slow rate but was at last complete...I can hardly see how anyone ought to wish Christianity to be true, for if so, the plain language of the text seems to show that the men who do not believe...will be everlastingly punished. And this is a heinous doctrine."***

(quoted by Paul Martin, *The Healing Mind: The Vital Links Between Brain and Behavior, Immunity and Disease,* 1997, p. 327)

Those endlessly unbelieving humans could be us; Darwin caters to that feeling because, as mortals, we would tend to share his aversion against such cruel punishment. However, we would not identify similarly with souls.

Both Malachi scriptures tell that the flesh will turn to stubble and be ashes under our feet.

(Malachi 4:1): And all the proud, yes, all who do wickedly will be stubble. And the day which is coming shall burn them up," Says the LORD of hosts.

1

(Malachi 4:3): [3]You shall trample the wicked, for they shall be ashes under the soles of your feet On the day that I do this," says the LORD of hosts.

The Bible tells us that the flesh will die and become stubble when burned while the soul will suffer the eternal pain of the Lake of Fire.

However,

(Matthew 10) Also can be interpreted otherwise: [28] And do not fear those who kill the body but cannot kill the soul. But rather fear Him who is able to destroy both soul and body in hell.

In this case, "destroy" is meant to be mar, impair, deface, scar, injury, or harm but not the inference to kill or eliminate.

Luke 12:5 clarifies this observation. [5]"But I will show you whom you should fear: Fear Him who, after He has killed, has the power to cast into hell; yes, I say to you, fear Him!

Hades still means eternal fire and punishment, as stated in the Rich man and Lazarus parable; I.e., **being in torment in Hades.** God has explicitly stated through Scripture:

(Obadiah 1:15): [15]As you have done, it shall be done to you; Your reprisal shall return upon your own head. [16] For as you drank on My holy mountain, So shall all the nations drink continually; Yes, they shall drink and swallow, And they shall be as though they had never been: God's revenge for the treatment of Israel.

(Matthew 3:12): [12]His winnowing fan is in His hand, and He will thoroughly clean out His threshing floor, and gather His wheat into the barn; but He will burn the chaff [comment: Sinners souls] with unquenchable fire."

(Luke 3:17): [17]His winnowing fan is in His hand, and He will thoroughly clean out His threshing floor and gather the wheat into His barn, but the chaff [comment: <u>Sinners souls</u>] He will burn with <u>unquenchable fire.</u>"

Darwin's question is: "Who makes the judgment on real justice for a crime?" If One hears that they will end up in Hades, "the unquenchable fire," if they don't believe, -- whose fault is it if they end up there? Everyone has free will: – I would think people would think twice rather than being arrogant enough to believe there is no God and, therefore, incur the risk they may be wrong. Where do you think Hitler ended after killing millions of Jews? What punishment would have been appropriate for him? Who makes the rules on what is necessary? --- Darwin or other humans? I would imagine that eternity in Hades would be a better deterrent than any one-time punishment, providing the recipient believed there was a Hades. Although a believer does not have to worry, the Atheist rightfully does.

After converting to believers, some Atheists have said: *"I would rather be a Christian and be right than be an Atheist and be wrong."* The former offers hope; the latter provides none. To an Atheist, The tribulation will create many converts! Darwin's question appears to be a "terrible doctrine" to an Atheist.

## Old and New Covenant Blood Relationship

God had set up for His worship in the Old Testament, but an unclear vision of heavenly things to come, emphasizing that the blood of bulls and goats could not take away sin but implying that the ritual of shedding blood was necessary. Jesus Christ, in place of the sacrificial lamb, would give His blood for our <u>*redemption.*</u> (Hebrews 10:1-4) transitions us from the earthly shadow to the divine mission of Christ (Hebrews 9:11-14), shedding His blood on the Mercy Seat in His heavenly Sanctuary.

(Hebrews 9:11- 14) [11] But Christ came *as* High Priest of the good things to come, with the greater and more perfect tabernacle not made with hands, that is, not of this creation. [12] Not with the blood of goats and calves, but with His _own_ blood He entered the Most Holy Place once for all, having obtained redempti*on* *[for us KJV]*. [13] For if the blood of bulls and goats and the ashes of a heifer, _sprinkling the unclean, sanctifies_ for the purifying of _the flesh,_ [14] _how much more shall the blood of Christ,_ who through the eternal Spirit offered Himself without spot to God, cleanse your conscience from dead works to serve the living God?

Only through the **shedding of Christ's blood on the Mercy Seat** could the death of the Lamb of God take away the sinful violations of God's Law. However, we live in a realm, not a symbolic world. He wrote those laws on stone tablets, held underneath the Mercy seat in the Ark of the Covenant. As stated earlier, Christ's blood from His crucifixion must find its way to the Mercy Seat to redeem humanity. This last statement leads us to another question; if we are mere shadowy visions of heaven, was there an echoing event that sprinkled blood on the Mercy Seat during Christ's crucifixion? Remarkably the answer is YES! For close to 2600 years, no one knew the location of the Ark. Then, on January six, nineteen eighty-two, an exceptional Christian man named Ron Wyatt found the Ark of The Covenant. While there are many doubters, his story is as enticing a miracle as any found in the Bible.

Jesus's blood on the Mercy Seat redeems us and satisfies the Law's claims that demand the sinner's death; i.e., the wages of sin is death. The blood had to go on the Mercy Seat to meet those claims: there is no remission without shedding blood.

### The Old Covenant Procedure

It was a time when God prepared humankind for the Lord's return by providing a worship procedure defined by Him for Moses to deliver to the people. First, in a meeting with Moses on Mount Saini, God gave Moses the ten commandants written, by His finger, on stone tablets defining His laws for living without sin. Next, Moses placed those stone tablets in an ark that God called the Ark of the Covenant. He then presented God's expectations to his followers, who agreed to do what God asked. Then, in Hebrews 9:20-22, Moses sprinkles blood on his disciples to ratify that acceptance, using relevant items in the sanctuary and the Ark of the Covenant to approve their agreement.

> (Hebrews 9:20-22) [19] For when Moses had spoken every precept to all the people according to the Law, he took the *blood of calves and goats, with water*, scarlet wool, and hyssop, and sprinkled both the book itself and all the people [20] saying, "This is the blood of the covenant which God has commanded you." [21] Then likewise, he sprinkled with blood both the tabernacle and all the vessels of the ministry. [22] And *according to the Law, almost all things are purified with blood, and **without shedding blood, there is no remission; i.e., pardoning of sin.***

In the (OT), on the day of atonement for personal sins, the person would bring in their sin offering and kill it with their hands while confessing their sins; figuratively transferring them to the slain animal. Once a year, the High Priest would collect the life-giving blood from such a sacrificed animal, which he offered for himself and the people's sins *committed* in ignorance. The High Priest would sprinkle the ritual blood on various objects within the Holy of Holies and the sanctuary. It would include shedding blood on the Mercy Seat of the Ark of the Covenant *as the means of expiation [the act of making amends or reparation for guilt or wrongdoing, i.e., atonement];* for it *is* the blood *that* makes atonement for the soul.

> (Leviticus 17:11) [11] For the life of the flesh is in the blood, and I have given it to you upon the altar to make atonement for your souls; for it is the blood that makes atonement for the soul:

i.e., the **death of the sinner represented by the blood satisfies the claims of the Law.**

One might ask, does the above Scripture refer to animal blood or Christ's blood? Since it is in Moses's day, it would be animal blood. Animal blood would only *temporarily* cover the people's sins during this period. The priests annually would repeat the act on the day of atonement.

> (Hebrews 10:1-4) For the Law, having a shadow of the good things to come, *and* not the very image of the things, can never with these same sacrifices, which they offer continually year by year, make those who approach perfect. ² For then would they not have ceased to be offered? The worshipers, once purified, would have no more consciousness of sins. ³ But in those *sacrifices, there is* a reminder of sins every year. ⁴ *For it is not possible that the blood of bulls and goats could take away sins.*

## Old Covenant Summary

* The Mosaic law of the Old Covenant only covered Israel; the ten commandants covered everyone

* The sinner had to figuratively transfer the sin to an animal by killing it as he repented of his sin

* The High Priest, who repeats the sprinkling of animal blood annually on the Ark, bequeathed forgiveness to the sinner for the year – But it had to be

* The God-written Law on stone tablets, the Ten Commandments, resided in the Ark of the Covenant in the Holy of Holies.

* ***Sprinkling the sacrificial blood on the Ark satisfied the claims of the Law*** that demanded the life of the sinner

## The New Covenant (redemption of sin)

In the **New Covenant,** the person seeks forgiveness from Jesus Christ through prayer, often using the LORD's Prayer, which emphasizes the conditions of confession, repentance, and forgiveness. God had given His only Son to humanity. He replaced the Old Covenant sacrificial lamb in one event and accepted the world's sins by giving His life in the crucifixion.

(John 3:16) ¹⁶ For God so loved the world that He gave His only begotten Son, that whoever believes in Him should not perish but have everlasting life.

(1 Peter 1:18-19) ¹⁸ knowing that you were not redeemed with corruptible things, *like* silver or gold, from your aimless conduct *received* by tradition from your fathers, ¹⁹ **_but with the_ precious blood of Christ, as of a lamb without blemish and without** *spot.*

When Christ said He came to fulfill the Law, the Mosaic laws were fulfilled through His birth, death, and resurrection and became obsolete when God placed those rules in man's hearts and minds replacing the old with the new.

(Matthew 5:17) ¹⁷"Do not think that I came to destroy the Law or the Prophets. I did not come to destroy but to fulfill.

In preparing for the New Covenant, God tells Jeremiah:

(Jeremiah 31:33) ³³ But this is the covenant that I will make with the house of Israel after those *[comment: OT]* days, says the LORD: *I will put My Law in their minds, and write it on their hearts, and I will be their God, and they shall be My people.*

(Galatians 3:28) ²⁸There is neither Jew nor Greek, there is neither slave nor free, there is neither male nor female; *for you are all one in Christ Jesus.*

Therefore, the **New Covenant** is for all humanity, while the **Old Covenant** mainly covered Israel through the Mosaic Law. The blood from Jesus's crucifixion substituted for the sacrificed animal's blood: He became the Lamb of God and the Holy Priest and Mediator, pleading for His people's pardon based on His blood given at Calvary sprinkled on the Ark of the Covenant. Christ's *death perfects the Sanctified.*

(Hebrews 10:11-18) [11] And every priest stands ministering daily and offering repeatedly the same sacrifices, which can never take away sins. [12] But this Man, after He had offered one sacrifice for sins forever, sat down at the right hand of God, [13] from that time waiting till His enemies are made His footstool. [14] For by one offering He has perfected forever those who are being sanctified. [15] But the Holy Spirit also witnesses to us; for after, He had said before,

[16] "This *is* the covenant that I will make with them after those days, says the LORD: I will put My laws into their hearts, and in their minds, I will write them," [a] [17] *then He adds,* "Their sins and their lawless deeds I will remember no more." [b] [18] Now where there is remission, *there is* no longer an offering for sin.

**The New Covenant Procedure**

Under the New Covenant, the sinner confesses to sin in word, thought, and deed and repents their iniquities to ask Jesus for forgiveness. God has transferred His Laws to our hearts and minds in exchanging the Old Covenant for the New. Our Christian bodies now become the temple of the Holy Spirit, which God purchased with the blood of His Son. We have free will to select our life's path, so our conscience always will tell us whether we are sinful or not: the choices are ours to make. Following that thought, the Bible says that we must become "born again" to see the Kingdom of Heaven, meaning we will shed our sinful selves and spiritually become born again in the body of Christ. To achieve that, we must:

> **(Romans 10:9)** If you confess with your **mouth**, the Lord Jesus and believe in your heart that God has raised Him from the dead, you will be saved.

Finally, we must always ask Jesus to come into our hearts to guide us. Many different philosophies exist concerning the forgiveness of sins. Some believe that if one believes in Christ, that is all we need for

Salvation. Contrary to scriptural teachings, others will humanize the interpretation to align with their thoughts. My personal belief is that sin is a sin, is a sin. It requires repentance, along with asking for forgiveness. The message that called for repentance has not changed since John the Baptist. The Hades Road is broader than the One to heaven since many follow misguided interpretations.

As a casual Christian, I thought I would go to heaven without knowing the needed Godly steps of my journey. Now I believe if one trusts in Christ and fights the urges to sin, even if he fails, God's mercy will sustain them – to a point. Only God knows when that might be, and He might punish you. My journey has had some successes, but I am still a work in progress.

(Hebrews 13:20), [20]through the blood of the everlasting covenant

(2 Corinthians 3:11), what remains is much more glorious.

(2 Corinthians 3:6) [3]....written not with ink but by the Spirit of the living God, not on tablets of stone but tablets of flesh, that is, of the heart.

(1 Corinthians 6:19-20) [19] Or do you not know that your body is the temple of the Holy Spirit in you, whom you have from God, and you are not your own? [20] For you were bought at a price; therefore glorify God in your body[a] and in your Spirit, which is God's.

## The New Covenant Summary

*The New Covenant covers all humanity*

- *Christ became the sacrificial Lamb of God who gave His life for humankind **by shedding His blood on the cross.** The sinner repented and asked for forgiveness from Christ, the Lamb, to accept his sin.*

- Christ, the High Priest in heaven, became the mediator between the sinner and God.

- *In the Old Covenant, **to fulfill the claims of the Law, Christ would have to have His blood and water sprinkled on the actual Ark of the Covenant for the remission of sin***

- Coincident with His death, similar to the sprinkling occurring with animal blood right after the animal's passing., Jesus gave His blood for the sins of humanity.

- Man became the temple of God because God implanted the commandments in our minds and hearts along with the Holy Spirit.

- Somehow the ***Sprinkling of Christ's sacrificial blood on the Ark must have happened to satisfy the claims of the Law*** that demanded the sinner's life.

The remaining question is, how does Jesus's blood gets shed on the Mercy Seat of the Ark when for roughly 2600 years, no one knew where it was; -- until recently?

## The "Contentious" Promised Land

Why did God take the land from the *Canaanites* and give it to the Jews as the Promised Land? You would know if you had a compass based on God's word: The Canaanites were so sinful in our Father's eyes that they believed there was nothing they could not do. Therefore, they did not obey the tenets and commands of our LORD GOD. Instead, they did everything from child sacrifice to temple prostitution, worshiping multiple gods, bestiality, and any other perversion, etc., they could imagine. Not only that, but they knew God was aware of what they were doing and still were content to worship their many gods, not the GOD that counted. Because God's fury commanded Moses to tell Joshua to destroy all life, "everything that breaths" in the Canaanite cities, Joshua did; while this sounds extreme, we must realize that sin is like cancer. Satan is the destroyer, where the wages of sin are death, whereas the living God gives eternal life. There can be no compromise other than to ask the sinner to repent, relinquish their sin, and ask for forgiveness. Intermarriages into a sinful culture will spread that sin to vulnerable children unaware of what is happening. The Canaanites had an opportunity to change; they did not and, as a result, lost their land.

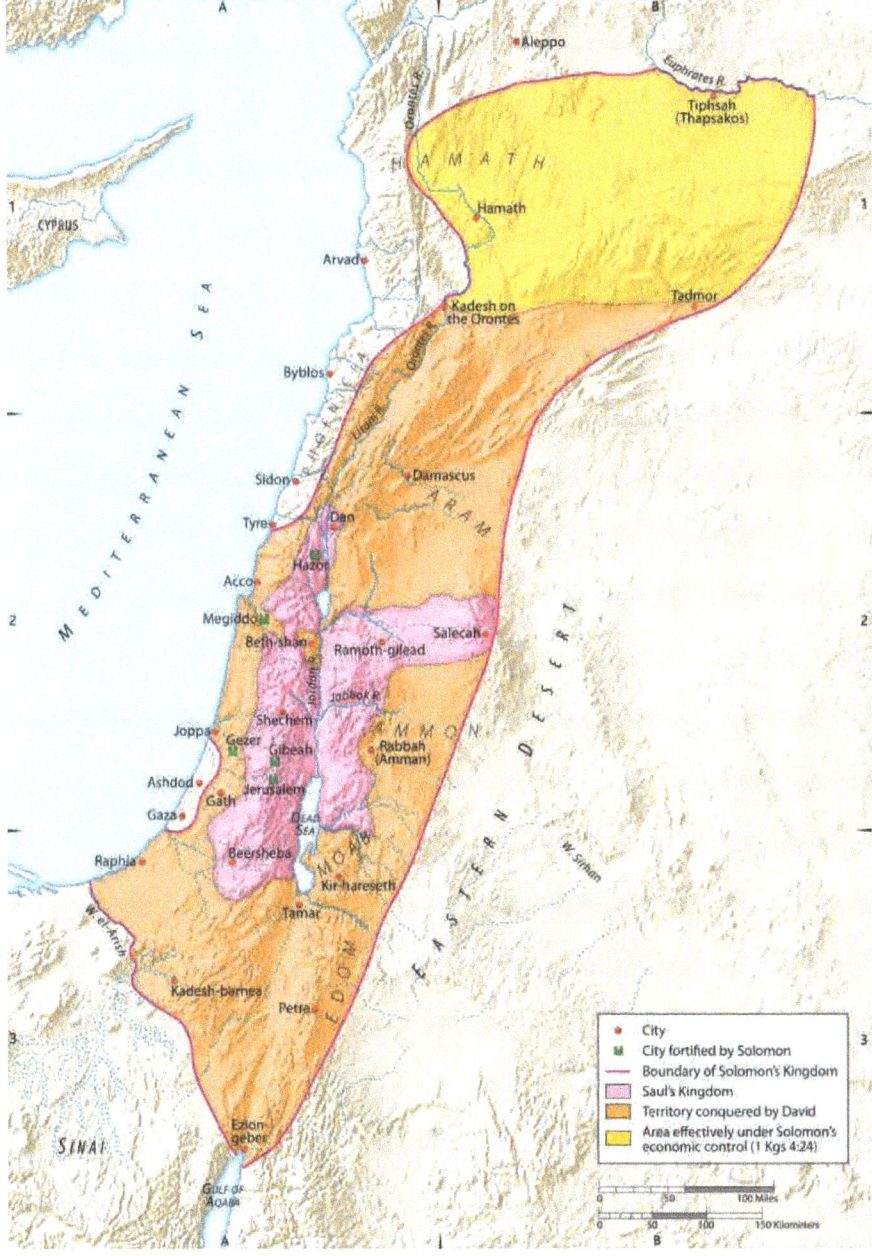

The story starts with the age-old debate concerning God's promise in His covenant with Abraham. The promised land of Canaan was a gift from God to Abraham and his descendants. The southern border is the spanned territory defined by a line connecting the Mediterranean going south through the Wadi River of Egypt, linking to Eilat's city at the Red Sea tip. The northern boundary will extend from the Great Sea or the Mediterranean through Lebanon and Syria to the Euphrates River north. The eastern border is a line from the Euphrates River in the north, extending south, past Damascus, along the slopes on the east side of Galilee. Today, the area is the Golan Heights; the boundary then returns to the Red Sea tip's starting point.

> (Deuteronomy 1:6-8): "The LORD, our God, spoke to us in Horeb, saying: You have dwelt long enough at this mountain. [7]Turn and take your journey, and go to the mountains of the Amorites, to all the neighboring places in the plain, in the mountains and the lowland, in the South and on the seacoast, to the land of the Canaanites and Lebanon, as far as the great river, the River Euphrates. [8]See, I have set the land before you; go in and possess the land which the LORD swore to your fathers—to Abraham, Isaac, and Jacob—to give to them and their descendants after them.

> (Amos 9:14-15): [14]I will bring back the captives of My people Israel; They shall build the waste cities and inhabit them; They shall plant vineyards and drink wine from them; They shall also make gardens and eat fruit from them.[15]I will plant them in their land, And no longer shall they be pulled up From the land I have given them, "Says the LORD your God."

God intended that Israel inherit the land within the borders and be fruitful and multiply as long as they obeyed the Mosaic Law. God would abundantly bless the nation but warned them that disobeying the Law would curse Israel. Israel does not entirely inhabit their "Promised Land" because it did not live up to God's expectations. What about the Arabs –

what did God give them? As recorded in the Bible, do they have a right to contest the land God presented them?

God focused so much on His chosen people; one may see the Arabs ignored in prophetic Scripture. He had blessed and promised all of Abraham's children would multiply like grains of sand and populate the earth, so they have. Many Arab countries are oil-rich but run by monarchies that do not share the wealth with their populations. Arab lineage starts with Abraham conceiving a child with Hagar, his wife's Egyptian handmaiden. Ishmael became the Son of Hagar as the result of that union. God promised To make Ishmael fruitful and multiply his descendants exceedingly, creating a "great nation" (Genesis 17:20). Through the ancestry of Ishmael and Esau, the Arab line would increase throughout the earth. Today, the Arab population is about 175 million people occupying a total area approaching 5.3 million square miles; – much of it oil-rich land.

In contrast, the Jewish state has about 4 million people in only about 8,000 square miles. It would seem that the Arabs got the better end of the deal, so why all the hatred? Blame a family matter: the lineage of Isaac, Joseph, David, etc., became God's chosen people. Isaac's seed would produce the Messiah, while the descendants of Ishmael or Esau would produce the Arabs and, most probably, the Antichrist.

## GODS VS SATAN

Realizing that the Antichrist's qualities are the antithesis of Christ's holiness, the following attributes of the Antichrist are the opposite:

- Eternal,
- Infinite,
- Self-existent,
- beyond human understanding,
- omnipresent,
- omniscience
- (all-knowing),
- incomprehensible,

- unchanging,
- all-powerful,
- is pure love,
- patient,
- Holy,
- judgmental,
- righteous,
- He is capable of jealousy and wrath against non-repentant sinners while capable of abundant Grace for those that love and obey Him.

> (Galatians 5:19-21) list those who would not inherit the kingdom of God.

## God's Desire

To Be with Us

The Bible tells us that the gate to heaven is narrow, while Hades's door is vast. We are all His children: His grief would be infinitely unbearable when, by their choice, most of His children send themselves to destruction because they would not accept His love or guidance. My kids' motivation must be to make sure they know what they must do to make it to heaven. The thought that should I be good enough to get there and some of my children did not, my pain would be equally unbearable. In comparison, God's pain, anguish, and grief would have to be indescribable.

### What He wants from us

As a believer in God, then what does He want? Specifically: That we become like Jesus in word and deed–

> (Romans 8:28-31): [28]and we know that all things work together for good to those who love God," to those who are the called according to His purpose. [29]For whom He foreknew; He also predestined to be conformed to the image of His Son, that He might be the firstborn among many brethren.[30]Moreover, whom He predestined, these He also called; whom He called, these He also justified;

and whom He justified, these He also glorified. [31]What then shall we say to these things? If God is for us, who can be against us?

(John 14:12-14): [12]"Most assuredly, I say to you, he who believes in Me, the works that I do he will do also; and greater works than these he will do, because I go to My Father. [13] And whatever you ask in My name that I will do, that the Father may be glorified in the Son. [14] If you ask] anything in My name, I will do it.

(John 14:15-23,15): [15]"If you love Me, keep My commandments.[16]And I will pray for the Father and He will give you another Helper, that He may abide with you forever— [17]the Spirit of truth, whom the world cannot receive, because it neither sees Him nor knows Him, but you know Him, for He dwells with you and will be in you. [18]I will not leave you orphans; I will come to you. [19] "A little while longer and the world will see Me no more, but you will see Me. Because I live, you will live also. [20]At that day, you will know that I am in My Father, and you in Me, and I in you. [21]He who has My commandments and keeps them, he loves Me. And he who loves Me will be loved by My Father, and I will love him and manifest Myself to him." [22]Judas (not Iscariot) said to Him, "Lord, how is it that You will manifest Yourself to us, and not to the world?" [23] Jesus answered and said to him, "If anyone loves Me, he will keep My word, and My Father will love him, and We will come to him and make Our home with him. [24]He who does not love Me does not keep My words, and the word that you hear is not Mine, but the Father's who sent Me.

The Bible tells us that we are God's children, and He wants our love, companionship, and obedience under His conditions.

(2 Corinthians 6:15-18): defines it best where the apostle Paul describes God's desire: [16]And what agreement has

the temple of God with idols? For you are the temple of the living God. As God has said: "I will dwell in them And walk among them, I will be their God, And they shall be My people." [17]Therefore, "Come out from among them And be separate, says the LORD. Do not touch what is unclean, And I will receive you." [18]"I will be a Father to you, And you shall be My sons and daughters, Says the LORD Almighty."

To that end, God provided believers with the indwelling Holy Spirit to be a Counselor to guide us.

(Acts 2:38): [38] Then Peter said to them, "Repent, and let every one of you be baptized in the name of Jesus Christ for the remission of sins, and you shall receive the gift of the Holy Spirit.

Unlike the Old Testament times, where any communication with God was through the priests and prophets, now we can reach Him through personal prayers with the indwelling Holy Spirit's help. However, unbelievers with hardened hearts did not have this gift, only those that accepted Christ. So how does one explain His other conditions?

Faith, Love, and Obedience:

Perhaps the best example of God's expectation for us is Abraham's response to God's request that he gives his Son, Isaac, as a human sacrifice to God.

(Genesis 22:2): [2] Then He said, "Take now your son, your only *son* Isaac, whom you love, and go to the land of Moriah, and offer him there as a burnt-offering on one of the mountains of which I shall tell you."

Abraham responded with immediate, unquestioning obedience, but he became assured of Abraham's deep love for Him and removed the request when God saw this. Abraham's obedience to God's request gave Him the glory He deserves and is an example to us all about how to glorify God. Abraham knew if he were to sacrifice Isaac, God would bring him back to life. God promised Abraham that Isaac's offspring "will be reckoned," meaning that Isaac must be alive to populate the earth with Abraham's seed.

Our message is that God expects immediate, unquestioning faith and obedience.

> (Romans 6:23): [23]For the wages of sin *is* death, but the gift of God *is* eternal life in Christ Jesus our Lord.

If we obey God and have faith in Jesus Christ, we have the promise of eternal life in Heaven with God: If not, we can expect an eternity in the netherworld. It is important to note that obedience or living a Christ-like life isn't a drudge. (That is the fundamental lie of Satan – See Genesis 3.) Obedience to Christ is finding our place in the grand scheme of things. It uses the part just as the engineer designed it. God created us to "love and enjoy him forever" [from the Westminster Shorter Catechism.]

# OUR SALVATION

The following two scriptures may be somewhat misguiding;

(John 3:16) says: that whoever *believes in Him* should not perish but have everlasting life. And (John 5:24) -- and *believes in Him*, who sent Me has eternal life.

They state that one only has to "<u>believe</u>" to be saved. For many years, I had accepted a simple definition of "believe," which proclaimed I believed in Christ, that He had existed and rose from the dead. However, that interpretation would be too narrow compared to the context of the rest of the Scripture. In this case, the word signifies embracing the complete Revelation in the gospels that describe Christ, including the necessity of obedience and letting Him guide your life. One cannot separate faith from obedience. We can only abide in Him and his love by keeping His commandments, thereby allowing a personal relationship with Him. The Bible provides criteria to remain in his Grace. Otherwise, as Jesus said, "we will get cast into the fire" without belief. However, if we have a checkered past of sin,

God still may choose to save us on judgment day through his infinite grace and mercy. At His crucifixion, Christ saved a criminal next to Him on the cross for defending Him against the other convicts hurling abuses saying, "Are you not the Christ? Save Yourself and us!" The other rebuked him and told Jesus, "remember me when You come in Your kingdom!" [43]Jesus replied, "Truly, I say to you, today you shall be with Me in Paradise."!"

So how are we guaranteed Salvation?: By becoming "born again." To receive the gift of Salvation, we must have faith and believe in Jesus Christ with a sincere and open heart. We must believe He was crucified, died, and rose from the dead to sit at the right hand of God after three days, particularly evils, while rejecting the "natural" inclination to be in control—thinking that we know what is best for our lives. Once we decide to let Jesus enter our hearts, His Holy Spirit begins a process that ultimately transforms us.

In a half-hearted attempt, it would not necessarily happen all at once. There are probably times when you will have to repent because of not being instantly able to overcome sinning habits. Life will not get any more comfortable, and we still will have to deal with our everyday problems and hardships. However, we will approach issues differently with our changed hearts and find real, lasting solutions this time. A loving relationship with Christ throughout our lives will allow Him to lead us and reveal truths we had never known before. Shocking facts will provide far more profound insights into life's problems than possible. Yet, even without entirely understanding these solutions, we will see that He guided us step by step to safety in a process called sanctification. This event happens when God converts us into the image of Christ by making us "a work-in-progress" that is only complete when we join Him in heaven. But the Almighty will achieve it.

> (Philippians 1:6): ⁶being confident of this very thing that He who has begun a good work in you will complete *it* until the day of Jesus Christ (His return and judgment).

We have discarded our old sinful nature to become a new person in Christ, so we are "born again." One's assumption that we qualified to be "born again" by expressing a rational belief in God and Christ but were casual in obeying Him would be false. We might have thought we were good enough. Instead, we need to experience a crisis of belief to ask ourselves, are we prepared to put in that constant effort to replace the old selves. The answer requires action and energy. God wants us to give ourselves, as a living sacrifice, by daily putting aside personal, worldly desires to follow Him instead, giving Him all our energy for His disposal while trusting Him to guide us. We do this out of love for Christ, whom we have invited into our hearts, grateful that His sacrifice has forgiven our sins.

## Born Again

God's eternal plan is to have many souls become believers in Him rather than Satan. To that end, humanity must become "born again" by shedding all sin and obeying the tenets and statues of our Lord. Achieving this goal is the most important event of our lives: it will ensure eternal life with God and Jesus Christ in His Heavenly Kingdom. It is why I am writing this book. The winnowing process will decide whether the "good" candidates meet the Biblical standard for being "born again," so the Heavenly Book of Life will include their names. We are all foreordained to go through this filtering process to see who will join His Son's millennial reign on earth or God in Heaven.

Scriptures stating we cannot enter the kingdom of heaven unless we are "born again" beg the question: what does that mean, and what must one do to reach that state. *When we commit our lives to Christ, we believe in Him and agree to live a righteous, holy life, obey Him and verbally ask Him into our hearts to guide us forever. Having done that, we will become "born again."* Our covenant with Him in our new life will naturally yield good works. If we have achieved that status on earth and continue living a Godly life, we have reserved our rapture ticket to heaven when we die.

The term "works" has caused some concern in religious circles that we are obliged to have "works" as well as "faith" to be saved: i.e., that we need "works" along with faith to enter heaven. However, James 2:14-17 claims that faith without works is dead, whereas Romans 3:28 states: [28]*For we hold that one is justified by faith apart from works of the Law.* James tells us that we must have faith plus works, but Romans says we are justified by faith alone. Do these scriptures not conflict?

Indeed, we must have faith in Christ's Salvation: but what about "works?" It all depends on the motivation that delivers the "good works." If we are in Christ, and He is in us, our good works become *a consequence* of our love and beliefs, *not an obligation.* The distinction is what man does for the love of God, and Christ in becoming "born again" underpins the creation of a changed life *that delivers good works.* Thus, we see not faith plus works *but good works because of faith. As the body without the Spirit is dead, faith, without works, is dead.* A Christian that cannot account for "good works" is not "born again."

> **(James 2:18)** But someone will say, "You have faith, and I have works." Show me your faith without your works, and I will show you my faith by my works.

> **(James 2:26)** [26]For as the body without the Spirit is dead, so faith without works is dead also.

We must be aware of all the Biblical prerequisites that one must meet in obedience and follow God's laws to qualify as "born again." All our "good works" will be zero if we misjudge. The terrible error is that we will believe we are "born again" but are not. Perhaps we may have forgotten to forgive, or we judged others, lied about people, or Satan has deceived us, etc. The list is long.

The road to heaven is narrow, whereas the One to Hades is just the opposite. I can relate because even at a very young age, in my twenties, while I was a "C" and "E" Christian, going to church maybe twice a year on Christmas and Easter, I felt that I would go to heaven. I was wrong. Therefore, the critical benchmark for Salvation is to understand the Biblical threshold. Christ must make that distinction, not you.

Compared to the 1st resurrection of all believers on Christ's return, the 2nd resurrection for the rest of the dead would not happen until the thousand years were over. God and Christ would destroy Satan by fire when released.

Then God and Christ would throw the Devil into the lake of fire to join the Antichrist and the False Prophet.

The rest of the dead would stand before God in the Great White Throne Judgment, waiting for sentencing according to their acts chronicled by *the Book* of Life. But if no names were there, Christ cast them into the Lake of Fire.

"What must I Do to Be Saved?" taken from "Walvrood" somewhat repeats the above. It is an excellent study on what it takes because understanding this is the book's primary mission. The repetition may clarify what may not have been apparent to some in the previous description. Somewhat paraphrased is his following work.

## Grace

In discussing God's beautiful plan of Salvation, the apostle Paul sums it up in three verses, "For it is Grace that saves, through one's faith and belief in Jesus Christ. — It is a gift of God — not for the good works one does, so one cannot boast of good deeds being responsible, but that God has generously bestowed His gift on us.

"Grace" saves us from going to Hades. While "Grace" has different meanings related to Salvation, it speaks of kindness bestowed on one who does not deserve it. In other words, Grace pours favor on those not justifying it. In Grace, the question is not whether a person deserves support or blessing, but only whether judgment qualified one for such a favor. Every instance mentioning Grace is entirely due to God's favor, not individual works, i.e., Good Deeds.

## Through Faith

God bestows grace on those who exercise faith in Jesus Christ. However, this introduces an appropriate question as to what faith means. To careful observers of today's churches, it is evident that many have made some outward profession of faith in Christ but never have been "born again.." Therefore, they need evidence to merit Salvation. How can one know whether he has put his faith in Christ or not? According to:

> (James 2:19) [19] You believe that there is one God. You do well. Even the demons believe — and tremble! From this passage, there is saving faith and faith that does not save, as evidence that even demons believe God exists, but they visibly do not experience Salvation for just that belief.

An unsaved person must understand that while he is a sinner, as all men are sinners, this constitutes only a part of his condemnation before God. One sin that prevents him from entering into Grace and favor of God is unbelief. Accordingly, he must understand that Salvation is by faith alone. He also needs instruction on the subject of righteousness. The scriptures show different kinds of justice, such as false worship of personal works. Scripture clarifies that any individual actions we offer as payment, even if worthy, do not qualify us for Salvation.

> (Isaiah 64:6) Says, ⁶ But we are all like an unclean *thing*, And all our righteousnesses *are* like filthy rags; We all fade as a leaf, And our iniquities, like the wind, Have taken us away.

The sinner must learn nothing short of God's righteousness that will allow him redemption.

### Through Belief and Commitment

One must consider Salvation and the required preparatory work of the Holy Spirit before Salvation. Merely agreeing with Biblical facts and mentally believing Christ died for the world's sins does not reach the acceptable threshold for the "Saving faith" needed for Salvation. In other words, rational belief without a commitment to having faith and trust in Christ without repenting when one fails to obey His laws is insufficient.

The sinner reaching to Christ should understand that it requires more than assent—it requires an act of the whole person. This action may involve the mind and the emotions, or sensibility, and most of all, it consists of the will. Faith is a step authorized by One's free will, i.e., committing oneself to faith in Christ.

Accordingly, faith in Christ is an act of the whole person in Scripture. It involves the work of the Spirit in the conviction of sin and righteousness and judgment, and it means God's providing special enablement to one spiritually dead to believe in Christ. This type of belief is what the Bible defines as "saving faith."

It must need one's action and an act of God to bring it to consummation. The Scriptures make it understandable that not faith plus works, but faith that produces works, results in an individual's Salvation. The Father must draw the seeking sinner to Him, for Jesus said;

> (John 6:44): [44] No one can come to Me unless the Father, who sent Me, draws him, and I will raise him up at the last day. There must be the convicting work of the Spirit, and then the person must respond by an act of his will, empowered by God, to put his trust in Christ as his Savior.

It requires a personal commitment to God and Jesus Christ by obeying them and repenting when we fall short by asking forgiveness and having faith and belief.

## GODS CONCERNS

### Religious Statistics

Christianity is the only religion offering a God who sacrificed his only begotten **Son to pay for humanity's sins. Eighty-five percent of the world population claims some** religious faith, but only 31 percent have selected Christianity.

Given a global population of about 7.3 billion in 2015, then 6.2 billion accounts for 85% that believe in some religion. The Christian percentage gives roughly thirty-one percent times 7.3 billion, which equals about 2.2 billion Christians. However, only half or about 1.1 billion meet the saving standard of being "born-again." This leaves (7.3-1.1) = 6.2 billion to go through the Tribulation. Pg 45 https://www.pewresearch.org/fact-tank/2017/04/05/christians-remain-worlds-largest-religious-group-but-they-are-declining-in-europe/

Muslim countries in the Mid-East comprise the largest group of nations not reached. Americans not identifying with religion continue to increase rapidly -- about 1% per year since 2007. Approximately one-fifth of the U.S. public – and a third of adults under 30 – are religiously unaffiliated today. This figure is the highest percentage ever seen in (Pew Research Religion & Public Life Project, 2010) Pew Research Center polling. So why is it so difficult to convince people that God is the best answer to all problems? All of us should ask ourselves that question. Especially troublesome is that the number of non-affiliated unbelievers is growing among the younger generations. http://joshuaproject.net/ global_statistics

## Atheism vs. Christianity

In 1927, The Atheist Bertrand Russell said in his "Why I am not a Christian" dissertation concerning the universe's existence: **"The idea that things must have a beginning is really due to the poverty of our imagination."**

With experience gained since that time, today's physicists would argue their "Big Bang Theory" against Russell's flawed deductive reasoning. It is a perfect example of future knowledge overturning past beliefs. That data would have driven a different conclusion if known in the past. Only God can predict what is and is not; unfortunately, atheists and other unbelievers choose not to believe. To repeat an earlier argument, one needs to know everything to deduce the truth about a subject one knows little. Ironically, only God fills that requirement.

Are these occurrences a product of evolution and random chance? --- I think not. How does evolution account for individuals that recognize right from wrong? --- If we are a product of randomness, how does that manifest itself into the structure and focus of Christianity that is alien to a random process. The process of natural selection selects organisms for survival based only on their behavior, what they do—not what they think and feel. Evolutionary theory can explain the origin of traits that have survival value and thus, cannot define man's mental state and the absolute essence of man. In other words, the theory of evolution cannot account for man's existence. Here, we deal with the biblical truth that God created us in His image; one may consider the thought flawed, but it is nonetheless true.

(Romans 8:22) [22] For we know that the whole creation groaneth and travaileth in pain together until now. Because God created us in His image, He gave us independence. We are not robots but instead choose to follow God of our free will.

God takes this risk because of His very nature. Life is the arena in which we choose to believe; in God's gracious offer of Salvation and life with God or to follow One's evil will and reap the consequences.

(Romans 6:23) [23]For the wages of sin is death, but the gift of God is eternal life through Jesus Christ our Lord. (1)

The question is, with free will, do we prefer God's or Satan's rule? To love God and Jesus takes work and commitment while Satan lets us do our own thing; that is why the path to Hades is vast. *"I like the benefits of Christianity, but I'm not sure I am ready to give up control and let God lead."*

Having been a Casual Christian, I can speak for myself. In my case, I think it was the reluctance to give my control to Christ and commit with my heart. Does this make a big difference? --- And the answer for me is: YES! -- An enormous difference. If the right words were there but not the genuine commitment, I could not prove from my experience that I could not change on my own. The answer is simple – without that commitment to Christ, one does not have the staying power to break those habits. If one does submit, one may get rid of them or develop the discipline to control them. It is not easy --- but what is? In my case, I have noticed a difference in myself. Anyone can make that change with faith and energy.

## Uncommitted Christian

What is an uncommitted Christian? My definition is one who intellectually believes in God and Jesus Christ but has not allowed them to enter their hearts. I held a humanized version of what I needed: but my perception was wrong. I did not know it was false. I know because I was one for many years.

As I have said, while single, I was one of those Christians; after all, I had faith and belief. Most of us have good instincts, believe we are kind, caring, empathetic, and go out of our way to help people, donate money, etc. When my wife and I married, we both felt strong enough to raise our children as Christians that we became regular Churchgoers. Things learned from several church excursions per year did not stick in my memory in my college days and early working career. Many competing opportunities attract attention to "self" rather than the Almighty in our mid and early adult years. Others have felt the same way at that point in their lifetime. What made me change my mind?

What we all go through is very subtle. When young and during our working careers, our lives revolve around ourselves carving a successful existence. During that trial, we seek fun in our youth, partying, finding our future partner, etc.-- all things innocent enough but can lead to trouble. God would like us all to be like Jesus - of course, that will not happen. So if living as a casual Christian is not sufficient: what is? Speaking for myself, I would have to point to the events in my Religious Biography that would make me call out to God in prayer due to health and other upcoming issues.

As my Religious Biography describes, several incidents opened my spiritual eyes regarding God. Many personal things happen to each of us that one does not often talk about – it either drives us toward God or away from Him. I was fortunate; many incidents moved me toward Him. The Bible, church, and weekly sermons describe God's story and the Gospel of Jesus Christ. We know many religious people in the church-- it shows, and I often wonder why they think as they do. How do people get so committed -- especially at a very young age?

One can somewhat gauge him or herself by asking, "How often a day do you think of God or even pray to Him?" If the answer is never, then you have answered your question. There is a reason that the Bible states that the road to heaven is very narrow, and the path to Hades is vast. In researching this subject, beliefs exist that only 2% to 50% of Christians will go to Heaven for not satisfying the Biblical requirements they need. Being an engineer, I tend to think about things statistically. Consider

God, your boss, and you, the employee. If in His place, what would you think of a person giving you only a couple of days a year of their time and interest --?: Christmas and Easter -- two days out of 365. Would you consider that person committed; no! Do you think God will answer your prayers when you mostly have ignored Him? Surprisingly the answer is "Yes," but we have to call out to Him, the beginning expression of "belief." God wants us all to be what Jesus described as "born again." We should sacrifice our sinful nature daily in a commitment to Christ by inviting Him into our hearts and then being fruitful by doing His bidding in what He has called us to do.

It all sounds simple enough, so why do we tend to ignore Him. Part of the answer is that if we have not reached that commitment to Him, we have not experienced what happens as that responsibility increases. For example, during my ongoing conversion from a casual Christian to a follower, I, for the first time, experienced the peace described in the Bible. During a Katherin Kuhlman healing service trip with friend Al, I discovered "*the peace that passes all understanding*." While it did not last, I never forgot it. It is worth repeating; the experience encouraged more faith and belief, and as I started reading the Bible, the peace returned.

### Sinning: Unintentional and Otherwise

As presumed Christians, the risk is that we often simplify the implications of sinning by not fully understanding or accepting the definition of obedience to God's word. We tend not to pay enough attention to a sinful world to notice when we step around the meaning without even thinking about it. For example, do we have burning resentments against anyone or not forgiven someone? Remember that if we do not forgive, God also will not forgive us – our free passage to heaven may become null and void. Do we lose our temper in driving or show impatience, etc.? Do we gossip about friends and coworkers? Are we in self-righteous anger with someone?

In my experience, I have found self-righteous anger to be the most damaging emotion. We feel hurt by the other person knowing what they said was wrong and "self-righteously" defending ourselves. As a result, the debate became heated, with both sides believing the other was not listening to them.

At this point, old wounds may bring up arguments that happened years before and add fuel to the fire with things said that had nothing to do with the original dispute's start. Unless one forgives the incident, it generates scar tissue in the relationship that will not go away unless one can honestly forgive and forget with God's direction. Why do we respond that way? God has made each of us uniquely original – some of us have tempers --- others do not. Unfortunately, I do. People react to situations differently based on their makeup. The Creator makes everyone with a different template, but we all seek to make our way in this life as we can in common with everyone else.

Understanding brings empathy and tends to mitigate the effects of the disagreement. However, some will have a wrong perception built on a previous experience and place unwarranted responsibility on that individual. Under these conditions, one needs a concentrated effort to do the right thing and follow God's will. Without that, things will only get worse. I have found that simple thought to remember when in a self-righteous argument is to try and think of how to solve the other person's problem rather than blame.

> (Mark 10:44-45): [44]And whoever of you desires to be first shall be slave of all. [45]For even the Son of Man did not come to be served, but to serve, and to give His life a ransom for many."

That leads to the possibility of dialog rather than a loathing resentment. The call is to love one another as Christ loves us. A further example is of two sisters that had been very close friends; they had a falling out due to reasons that, over the years, they could not even clearly remember. However, the relationship dynamics became tense as they drifted further apart. Both had a self-righteous opinion of the other person based on perception, -- not communication concerning what was bothering the other. Both would have been right in their insights had they been correct. It turns out both perceptions were wrong.

This condition had gone on for some years, with the cold relationship. Only after they forgave each other did their bond return to normal. The bitter truth was that the older sister tried to defend the younger one, but the younger sister entirely misread her intentions. Equally valid, the older sister also had misinterpreted conditions between them. Both were guilty and found out the truth when they forgave the other. The point is that the separation between the two existed for many years. Satan was in control of fanning the flames of anger during that time. Only when we follow God's rule of forgiveness is the problem solved. During the conflict, each may have felt that they were candidates for going to Heaven. However, by God's rules, should either pass away without forgiving the other, that person may not have made it.

What are the odds of correctly analyzing an interpersonal conflict without talking to the other person and going just on One's perception? In my experience, it rarely works. We live in a sinful world, and if one's orientation is toward "self" rather than God, our reactions will tend to follow Satan's input. Ask yourself, "How many times a day do you think of God and thank Him for your blessings?" When I was younger and more interested in myself, I would have to say never. As I have aged and become more connected to God and changed, my answer is many times. As my extreme anger has diminished, my health has dramatically improved; I no longer take the Lord's name in vain – I may slip once or twice a year. I have never had the peace of mind that I now do. One should realize that these changes were only possible in becoming closer to the LORD.

> (1 Corinthians 1: 31) [31]that, as it is written, "He who glories, let him glory in the LORD."

There are a million ways to show disobedience without even thinking about it. There is no such thing as a bit of sin if one also believes such a thing was allowed. Under whose influence am I acting, the Casual Christian must ask himself? The unbeliever seemingly has no such problem and thinks he works under his cognizance of whatever he believes. The Bible would tell him otherwise and suggest he is under the power of this sinful world. The following self-test will give both the unbeliever and the Casual Christian a Biblical means to tell them what is needed to become a Christian if they are interested.

Taken from "**Are You A Christian.**"

Going to church does not make you a Christian, nor does one say a prayer, go down an aisle, pass a catechism, and tell yourself that you are trying to be a decent person. According to the scriptures, you can only be a Christian if Christ is in you, tested and proven.

God gives us instructions on how to "check ourselves" in Scripture. These cluster into five broad categories: 1) *Gospel Belief and Confession;* 2) *Born Again / Sonship / Correction*; 3) *Repentance / Deliverance from Sin*; 4) *Good Works by Grace*; 5) *The Fruit of the Spirit*. The first three are starting points but can also serve as ongoing tests, as we will see. The last two are living proof of "Christ Jesus in us," or not. These scriptures should encourage true Christians and cause a sober reflection on those who think they are but are not. http://www.acts17-11.com/christian.html

Each of the above categories offers many studies we could pursue to determine the truth, whether one is a Christian or not. The point is that we should each decide for ourselves. If it were any consolation, the apostle Paul suffered the same problem we all do. Paul told us:

> (Romans 7:15-20): [15]For what I am doing, I do not understand. For what I will do that I do not practice; but what I hate, that I do. [16]If then, I do what I will not do. I agree with the Law that it is good. [17]But now, it is no longer I who do it, but sin dwells in me. [18]For I know that in me (that is, in my flesh), nothing good dwells; for to will is present with me, but how to perform what is good I do not find. [19]For the good that I will do, I do not do; but the evil I will, not do, that I practice. [20]Now, if I do what I will not do, it is no longer I who do it, but sin that dwells in me.

The Casual Christian's question is, do you consider yourself a Christian just because you are a decent person and occasionally attend church? -- I felt that way for many years!

> (Romans 10:8-13): "The word is near you, in your mouth and your heart" [a](that is, the word of faith which we preach): 9 that if you confess with your mouth the Lord Jesus and believe in your heart that God has raised Him from the dead, you will be saved. 10 For with the heart, one believes unto righteousness, and with the mouth, confession is made unto Salvation. 11 For the Scripture says, "Whoever believes on Him will not be put to shame." [b] 12 For there is no distinction between Jew and Greek, for the same Lord over all is rich to all who call upon Him. 13 For "whoever calls on the name of the LORD shall be saved.

We must believe the true Gospel about the right One. The Christian life starts with embracing the Gospel, but what we accept as valid is also an ongoing test. Scripture warns us it is dangerous to drift away from one's faith as we go through life. Do we believe in, and are we following, the pure and scripture-defined Gospel of Jesus Christ? Going through the test should give a person insight to challenge their relationship with Christ.

Paul's previous statement, in Romans 7:15-20, says it all. At one time or another, we have all suffered lapses of control that result in losing our temper, and right after it happens, to ask ourselves, "why did we do that?"; and admonish ourselves. Assuredly, I have been one of those offenders. Most people consider themselves "decent" even though living among sinful surroundings perpetually tempts them to do bad things. Knowing the Savior alone, without focused action to obey Him, is insufficient. In my case, I have suffered lapses resulting in resentment, lack of forgiveness, impatience, anger, experienced anxiety, health, fears, etc. It is no different from the human condition that everybody else has faced.

I know I am preaching to the choir ---- we have all been in similar situations under different circumstances. Making these statements is not an attempt to show me as a paragon of virtue ---- far from it. Looking back at my changes over the years, I had success only since committing my life to Christ. He overcame many of my listed shortcomings giving me complete peace of mind. My biggest regret is that I had not realized this at a far younger age. I would not be writing this book without His power. After all, as the old bumper sticker noted, "Christians are not perfect, just forgiven."

Reflecting on my journey, I can now understand the difficulties of the road traveled when much younger, --It lacked a perspective that only can come with age. As a more youthful, casual Christian, I did not appreciate the additional rewards that could come with greater faith. However, experience has shown me that we embrace increased, rewarding experiences when we develop. As they happen, a person becomes aware of the possibility and becomes even more energized in their faith. Atheists, instead, seek contradicting arguments against those defending their faith. God demands that we first accept the Gospel as correct to receive His proofs. Contrary to all his beliefs, for a Christian to tell a skeptic about their truths, he cannot relate, believe, or understand what you are saying. Your proofs have no meaning to them, no matter how logical are your arguments.

For anyone familiar with the Bible, it should come as no surprise that severely stressful conditions periodically challenge unbelievers and Christians in a manner that invites them to call out to God in prayer. Many atheists and lukewarm Christians have reacted appropriately by seeking a stronger relationship with the Almighty. Unfortunately, the sinful world we live in uses the same events to hook us into an indulgent solution that becomes addictive. Free will, anchored in "Self," makes the wrong decision --- "Free will" that anchors in "Christ" gives the right One. Those who have become "hardcore" unbelievers will instead blaspheme and curse the LORD for creating their conflict. Instead, it may become their personal "crisis of Belief," changing their lives, for better or worse, depending on the decision. The unbeliever has an impossible task—

somehow, against all instincts, he must believe, for an instant, and ask, "God are you there?"— To find out whether He will answer or not.

So, it is with Nations. When a country shows such disregard for God that it progressively starts writing its laws to embrace Biblical sin, that land will open itself to punishment. It took Noah 100 years to build his "Ark." He would preach repentance to the people around him to avoid the flood he knew. They had one hundred years to believe and repent; they did not. Because "no one in the whole world except the eight members of Noah's family believed or repented," the flood came. Is our civilization reaching the same state? I think it has we are in the "times of the sorrows" just before the Tribulation described in Daniel's book.

# THE BIBLE

The Bible is a historical narrative. It is the individual record of God's revelation of himself to humanity, with the culmination of that Revelation being Jesus Christ. Evidence abounds that the Bible is historically accurate if not complete. Furthermore, much of the narrative is a story and poetry. Interpreting Biblical content is a challenge for the reader. A literal interpretation of the Bible is preferred unless a metaphorical, symbolic, or analogous explanation is more fitting. The "Blind Men and the Elephant" poem describes how people often discuss the Bible on whether it is God's word or the mistaken fallible meanderings of the human mind. It is a warning to be careful of one's interpretations.

## BLIND MEN AND THE ELEPHANT

Poem by John Godfrey Saxe (1816–1887)

*It was six men of Indostan to learning much inclined, Who went to see the Elephant (Though all of them were blind), That each by observation Might satisfy his mind.*

*The First approached the Elephant And, happening to fall Against his broad and sturdy side, At once began to bawl: "God bless me! But the Elephant Is very like a wall!"*

*The second feeling of the tusk, Cried, "Ho! what have we here So very round and smooth and sharp? To me, 'tis mighty clear This wonder of an Elephant Is very like a spear!"*

*The Third approached the animal, And happening to take The squirming trunk within his hands, Thus boldly up and spake: "I see," quoth he, "the Elephant Is very like a snake!*

*The Fourth reached out an eager hand And felt about the knee. "What most this wondrous beast is like Is mighty plain," quoth he; 'Tis clear enough the Elephant Is very like a tree!"*

*The Fifth, who chanced to touch the ear, Said: "E'en the blindest man Can tell what this resembles most; Deny the fact who can This marvel of an Elephant Is very like a fan!"*

*The Sixth no sooner had begun About the beast to grope Than, seizing on the swinging tail*

*That fell within his scope, "I see," quoth he, "the Elephant Is very like a rope!"*

*And so these men of Indostan Disputed loud and long, Each in his own opinion Exceeding stiff and strong, Though each was partly in the right, And all were in the wrong!*

**Moral:** *So oft in religious wars, The disputants, I wean, Rail on in utter ignorance Of what each other mean, And prate about an Elephant Not one of them has seen!*

This poem implies that if we analogously consider the Bible the elephant, we must study and read it many times to get an accurate insight into its teaching. Nowhere is this story more accurate than the interaction between science and the Bible. The scribes and apostles wrote the Bible to tell God's story. Likewise, the workings of creation are gradually exposing themselves through science. Human reason, though, with its limited capability, cannot explain or show God because of His infinite nature. It also cannot tell the beginnings of nor the why of creation. Only scripture can teach these things. With this understanding as an assumption, the more we learn about science, the more we know God's majesty and greatness. The impulse to include this poem came early one morning, thinking that the Bible is complex and can cause many interpretations. Discernment only comes with studying the "Word." However, the main point is to accept the gospel message of believing in God and Jesus Christ and committing oneself to them with the explicitly stated reasoning in the Bible. Misperceptions of atheists and partial believers abound at every level. As an example:

> (Luke 14:26): [26]"If anyone comes to Me and does not hate his own father and mother and wife and children and brothers and sisters, yes, and even his own life, he cannot be My disciple.

Atheists often take such scripture literally rather than metaphorically, i.e., "How could people defend following a God that asks them to hate their family?" In this example, 'Scripture is comparing the difference in the needed love for Christ to hypothetically hating your family (whom you love) that would be necessary to follow him. A more straightforward way of making the comparison would be to say that if one likes their family a specific amount, we would need a vastly more significant amount of love for Jesus to follow Him. Without that increased level of commitment, it would be impossible. He counsels that if that were to be the case, it would be better not even to try to be His disciple rather than look foolish in a failed attempt.

### Biblical Message

One could best state the overall Biblical message using:

> (Matthew 13:44-52): **The Parable of the Hidden Treasure** [44] "Again, the kingdom of heaven is like treasure hidden in a field, which a man found and hid; and for joy, over it, he goes and sells all that he has and buys that field.
>
> #### The Parable of the Pearl of Great Price
>
> [45] "Again, the kingdom of heaven is like a merchant seeking beautiful pearls,[46] who, when he had found one pearl of great price, went and sold all that he had and bought it.

If we are searching for the kingdom of heaven and learning what it takes to get there, we must be willing to give up everything to achieve that goal. The Bible tells us that one must commit their heart, soul, and mind to follow Jesus Christ to enter the kingdom of heaven.

## The Parable of the Dragnet

> [47]"Again, the kingdom of heaven is like a dragnet that was cast into the sea and gathered some of every kind, [48] which, when it was full, they drew to shore; and they sat down and gathered the good into vessels, but threw the bad away. [49]So it will be at the end of the age. The angels will come forth, separate the wicked from among the just, [50]and cast them into the furnace of fire. There will be wailing and gnashing of teeth." [51]Jesus said to them,[a] "Have you understood all these things?" They said to Him, "Yes, Lord." [52]Then He said to them, "Therefore every scribe instructed concerning[c] the kingdom of heaven is like a householder who brings out of his treasure *things* new and old."

However, God's heavenly dragnet will pull in both sinners and believers to face His judgments; if we do not heed God's advice, an eternity in the abyss awaits us. We must be sure that, as believers, we have the necessary "born again" beliefs to avoid the fate of the wicked. As residents of heaven, we must witness Christ by teaching others about the kingdom so they can appreciate the value of the treasure and realize what it takes to find it. Reiterating the question of "who will enter the Kingdom of Heaven," the dividing line is those who DO the Father's will. Jesus describes a true disciple as one who believes in Him and does His will - John 8:30-32. Salvation by grace demands the necessity of obedience.

Let us not mistakenly think that we have a free ticket to heaven because we "believe" in Jesus! Salvation is by grace, not what we may consider exemplary works while thinking we are obeying God but are not. Jesus will likewise not recognize us doing things for which we had no authority: i.e. Something we are doing on wrong assumptions separate from the will of God. Although one may consider themselves religious, doing many things in the name of Jesus, still He can say: "I never knew you; depart from Me..." Tit 3:3-7. Obeying God is more complicated than we may suspect. As Jesus said,

> (Matthew 7:21): [21]"Not everyone who says to Me, 'Lord, Lord,' shall enter the kingdom of heaven, but he who does the will of My Father in heaven.

> (James 1:22-25): [22]But be doers of the word, and not hearers only, deceiving yourselves. [23]For if anyone is a hearer of the word and not a doer, he is like a man observing his natural face in a mirror; [24]for he observes himself, goes away and immediately forgets what kind of man he was. [25]But he who looks into the perfect law of liberty and continues in it and is not a forgetful hearer but a doer of the work, this one will be blessed in what he does

> (Roman 6:17-18): Christ is the author of salvation to all who obey Him –(He 5:9) Christ will come in judgment against those who obey not the gospel.

http://executableoutlines.com/matt/mt7_21.htm **Executable Outlines, Copyright © Mark A. Copeland, 2011**

What must we abide by to satisfy our Father's will? It begins with:

a. Repentance toward God and faith in Jesus Christ - Ac 20:21
b. Confessing Jesus as Lord - Rom 10:10
c. Being baptized into Christ for the remission of sins - Ac 2:38 -- Followed by a life of faithful service to Christ, confessing one's sins along the way - Re 2:10; 1Jn 1:9

The catch is that we truly understand the meaning of obedience and faith to eliminate our misinterpretation of those definitions, so unintentional sinning does not trap us.

## Truth?

Most dangerous is that anyone can perceive that will often be wrong. Observation accuracy is inversely proportional to the amount of research and effort put into studying the target of our interest. Misinterpreting scripture by presuming opinions too early can lead us to believe something untrue. Literal truths lie in the metaphors, analogies, parables, and parallel scriptures that tell the Bible's story. Searching for patterns within this jungle of Biblical data that will provide different looks at the same information from a different perspective will give a complete vision of the truth.

Because of the above, even Biblical scholars have differing opinions on making this type of interpretation. Moreover, it leads to many opposing theories of scriptural meaning, especially in Daniel and Revelation's prophecies. Thus, the question of what information tells us becomes a complex one. An adage is appropriate:

1. a fool is "one who knows not _but knows not that he knows not,_"

2. versus

3. a wise man "knows not "_but knows that he knows not._"

The previous definition distinguishes what we know or do not about what we do not know. Science is the determined march, from lack of knowledge to comprehension. The knowledge's accuracy must come from hypothesizing cause and effect scenarios and determining what is correct by devising tests to prove or disprove their theories: I.e., methodically making progress using a keen understanding of what man knows and does not. As we shall see, the Bible often points the way for science to "get it right." Such is the case for the Biblical claim that God created the universe from nothing—long before science would discover that fact with their "Big Bang Theory." They could not accept and still cannot; God is the Creator, and His word is all-powerful.

# THE TRUSTWORTHINESS OF THE BIBLE:

Why should we trust the Bible? After all, humans wrote it, so why would it not just be a reconstruction of ancient mythology. What about the other religious books: the Quran, the Book of Mormon, etc., are they equally suspect? What makes the Bible any different from the other holy books? As Christians, we need to be able to answer these questions.

Charlie Campbell in "Can We Trust the Bible?" http://www.alwaysbeready.com/bible-evidence?id=99

Prophecy of the Bible is nothing more than God's omniscient certainty of future happenings reported through the prophets. None of the other notable twenty-six sacred books, which religious people believe were also divinely inspired, contain any explicitly fulfilled prophecies, "none." The following example, "*Or* shall a nation be born at once?" Isaiah 66:8, given by Israel's rebirth in 1948, with many examples. To date, 100% of all the prophecies have come true. Why should this be the case?; because of His 100% predictive accuracy, this alone proves His existence. Humanity's greatest mistake would be to make a God of their choosing, "in their image," because he does not want to be accountable to Him, the real God. The Old Testament prophesied that Jesus would be born of the seed of Abraham:

> (Isaiah 9:6): [6]For unto us a Child is born, Unto us, a Son is given, And the government will be upon His shoulder. And His name will be called Wonderful, Counselor, Mighty God, Everlasting Father, Prince of Peace.
>
> (Romans 9:7-9): [7]nor are they all children because they are the seed of Abraham; but, "In Isaac, your seed shall be called." [8]That is, those who are the children of the flesh, these are not the children of God, but the children of the

promise are counted as the seed. ⁹For this is the word of
promise: "At this time I will come, and Sarah shall have
a son."

Isaiah lived from approximately 740-698 BC and made the above
prophecies, while the apostle Paul wrote Romans' book about 56-57 AD.
Can one read the above descriptions and not be in awe that they correctly
predict Christ's coming from Isaac's lineage in Isaiah and then reaffirm it
happened in Romans?

No archeological discovery has ever overturned a Biblical reference.
Scores of archeological findings confirm in clear outline or with an
exact detailed historical statement in the Bible. Needless-to-say proper
evaluation of Biblical descriptions has often led to surprising discoveries."
[Nelson Glueck, Rivers in the Desert, p. 31.] (Glueck) These are words
of a man credited with uncovering more than fifteen hundred ancient
sites in the Middle East. ["Archaeology: The Shards of History," Time,
December 13, 1963].

They found a limestone block about three feet tall and two feet wide
that had been turned upside down and reused as part of a flight of steps
during one of the theater's renovations. It bore an inscription in Latin,
mentioning "Pontius Pilate, Prefect of Judea."

Discovered in the town of Dan, a little north of the Sea of Galilee in
Israel. The inscription, written in Aramaic by Israel's enemies, describing
the loss of the kings of Judah and Israel, mentioned "the king of Israel"
and the king of the "House of David." It was a fantastic discovery and
helped verify that David was an actual historical figure for the first time.

Biblical authors wrote Scripture in three different languages: Hebrew,
Aramaic, and Greek. When we ask 40 people from 60 generations and
three different continents who speak three other languages to write 66
documents regarding life's most controversial questions: one would
expect some serious problems. Moreover, that book would be supposed
to be a challenging read. Irrespective of these factors, the Bible is an
entirely harmonious, coherent account of God's attempts to reconcile

sinners back to Him: through His Son, Jesus Christ. This internal consistency is extraordinary evidence that the Bible's authors were guided by the Holy Spirit when they wrote the Bible's different books. Naturally, one could give many more examples of Biblical truth, but the need for further evidence is not essential if the above examples convince you. My Christian friends and I believe in God and Jesus Christ strictly by exposure to the Gospel and need no other evidence that the Bible is true; atheists and unbelievers still need proof.

## FULFILLED PROPHECY

For unbelievers, it seems, there is an arrogant tendency to proclaim the impossibility of God because they fit the definition; "None is so blind who will not see." The inability to scientifically prove God's existence automatically triggers the "He does not exist" mantra. Unbelievers quickly dismiss the Bible's truths with a hand wave for thousands of years. Also, they ignore the newest prophecy to come true --

The signed termination of the British Mandate with a pen stroke at midnight fulfilled Isaiah 66 on 14 May 1948 and created Israel.

> (Isaiah 66:7-8): [7] "Before she was in labor, she gave birth; Before her pain came, She delivered a male child. [8]Who has heard such a thing? Who has seen such things? Shall the earth be made to give birth in one day? Or shall a nation be born at once?

> (Ezekiel 37:21-22): [21]"Then say to them, 'Thus says the Lord God: "Surely I will take the children of Israel from among the nations, wherever they have gone, and will gather them from every side and bring them into their own land; [22]and I will make them one nation in the land, on the mountains of Israel; and one king shall be king over them all; they shall no longer be two nations, nor shall they ever be divided into two kingdoms again.

# INTRODUCTION: Astronaut gods?

Some 445,000 years ago, astronauts from another planet came to Earth searching for gold. Splashing down in one of Earth's seas, they waded ashore and established Eridu, "Home in the Faraway." In time, the initial settlement expanded to a full-fledged Mission Earth -- with a Mission Control Center, a spaceport, mining operations, and even a way station on Mars. Short of a workforce, the astronauts employed genetic engineering to fashion Primitive Workers-Homo sapiens. The Flood that catastrophically swept the Earth required a fresh start; the astronauts became gods, granting Mankind civilization and teaching it to worship. Then, about four thousand years ago, all achievements unraveled in a nuclear calamity. The visitors brought it about on Earth during their rivalries and wars.

How do we account for such stories? After all, *Paleoanthropologists* found ancient skeletal remains of a jawbone in Ethiopia that they dated *2.8-million-years-old*. It is the oldest fossil in ancient human history by more than 400,000 years. The Discovery of Neanderthal skeletons worldwide shows us that some people existed thousands, if not millions, years before Adam and Eve. Extraction of DNA from bone samples has demonstrated inbreeding between humans and Neanderthals begs the question: What was the difference between Neanderthals and Adam and Eve's creation?

As a Christian, I believe God started creating human prototypes very early, as soon as Earth could support life. Neanderthals were somehow different from Adam and Eve. I suspect God created Adam and Eve to answer Satan's attempt to contaminate the human DNA and gene pool with his fallen angels sinfully mating with earth's women. Nephilim Giants were proof of that corruption. Today, everyone living outside of Africa has a small amount of Neanderthal in them, carried as a living relic of these ancient encounters. A scientific team comparing the two species' complete genomes concluded that most Europeans and Asians have between 1 to 4 percent Neanderthal DNA. https://genographic.nationalgeographic.com/neanderthal/

Perhaps the following scripture starts to provide an answer with God's story of those pre-Adam and Eve days.

> (Genesis 6:1-8): Now it came to pass when men began to multiply on the face of the earth, and daughters were born to them, [2] that the sons of God saw the daughters of men, that they were beautiful, and they took wives for themselves of all whom they chose. [3] And the LORD said, "My Spirit **shall not strive[a] with man forever, for** he is indeed flesh; yet his days shall be one hundred and twenty (Jubilee?) years" [4] *There were giants (Nephilim) on the earth in those days, and also afterward, when the sons of God came into the daughters of men, and they bore children to them. Those were the mighty men who were of old, men of renown.* [5] *Then the LORD saw that the wickedness of man was great in the earth and that every intent of the thoughts of his heart was only evil continually.* [6] *And the LORD was sorry that He had made man on the earth, and He was grieved in His heart.* [7] *So the LORD said, "I will destroy man whom I have created from the face of the earth, both man, and beast, creeping thing and birds of the air, for I am sorry that I have made them."* [8] *But Noah found grace in the eyes of the LORD.* (8)

Further clarifying heavenly relationships:

> Matthew 22:30 states that for men and women in heaven: "For in the resurrection, they neither marry nor are given in marriage, but are like angels of God in heaven."

This answer Jesus gave to the Sadducees concerning their question of marriage in heaven. However, the implication is that angels in paradise usually follow the rule restricting marriage, but it does not necessarily apply to the fallen angels.

(Luke 20:35-36): further clarifies [35] But those who are counted worthy to attain that age, and the resurrection from the dead, neither marry nor are given in marriage; [36] nor can they die anymore, **for they are equal to the angels and are sons of God.** (4)

So the conclusion up to this point is that the fallen angels, fallen sons of God, somehow did mate with mortal women and gave birth to giants.

While the pre-Adamic population of Sumeria may have believed the equivalent of Astronautics descended on them, the Bible would tell you that these were the fallen angels accompanying Lucifer when God evicted them from heaven. Speculation would have us believe this happened somewhere between the creation of Earth and Adam and Eve. One might ask: Why was he removed? There was an epic battle between God and Lucifer (Satan) sometime before God created Adam and Eve. Lucifer caused and lost that battle because he defied God to become like Him. The result: God tossed him, and those Angels siding with him, down to earth. We know because Satan was already in the Garden of Eden when God created Adam and Eve. The Sumerian story's introduction suggests that God cast Lucifer and his fallen angels down about 445,000 years ago; they were the so-called astronauts from outer space. Since the Bible covers our present age, there is not much detail in that previous period except the brief message describing the result of the early battle between God and Lucifer.

(Isaiah 14:12-15): How you have fallen from heaven, morning star, son of the dawn! **You have been cast down to the earth,** you who once laid low the nations! [13]**You said in your heart, "I will ascend to the heavens;** I will raise my throne above the stars of God; I will sit enthroned on the mount of assembly, on the utmost heights of Mount Zaphon [14]**I will ascend** above the tops of the clouds; **I will make myself like the Most

**High.**" [15]But you are brought down to the realm of the dead, to the depths of the pit.

One can only speculate on God's motive in turning Satan loose on earth with his fallen angels. But given that He has allowed Satan a certain degree of freedom to tempt humanity into sinfulness, perhaps that is the answer. After all, He will also permit the Antichrist in our generation to do the same. These fallen angels from heaven had extensive divine knowledge to achieve many wondrous things: maybe even moving monoliths, building pyramids, etc.

Perhaps, even then, after being evicted from heaven, God gave Satan his chance to prove that he and his fallen angels could do a better job than He. Back then, the same battles for man's soul were no different than they are now. After the fall, Adam and Eve's appearance may create grounds to ask, who were the people who pre-dated them – I thought man started with Adam and Eve?

The early Sumerian society arose during the Neolithic or New Stone age Period, between 10,200 BC and 4,500 and 2,000 BC. Therefore, it existed between the pre-Adamic age starting around 8000BC and Adam and Eve's creation around 4000 BC.

Sumeria's initial population would have been the early stone age humanoids that did not have the same DNA and gene pool as Adam and Eve.

Religion evolved from the humanity of that time from watching the stars, attributing everything to various Gods because they knew no better. The essential point is that some spiritual awareness existed. However, Polytheism was the only religion in ancient Mesopotamia for thousands of years before other faith and Christianity influenced those beliefs. So, from the outset, with the worship of multiple gods, one can assume that Satan was in control, and their actions reinforced the notion. As an early civilization that suddenly received many advanced god-like creatures, the population, not surprisingly, presumed they were Gods.

What these fallen angels did firmly places them in Satan's camp. They mated with mortal women and, as a result, created giants on the earth called the Nephilim.

> Genesis 6:1-2 Now it came to pass when _men began to multiply_ on the face of the earth, and _daughters were born to them_, ²that the _sons of God saw_ the _daughters of men_, that _they were beautiful;_ and they took wives for themselves of all whom they chose.

The fallen angels could no longer retain their heavenly bodies, thus becoming flesh and blood and capable of procreating with the beautiful daughters of earthly man-producing giants, the Nephilim.

The opinions questioning how this mating occurs stimulate never-ending debates. Because of the lack of knowledge, they lead to pure speculation. Suffice it to say, angels did come down, scripture states it happened -- and we discovered giants to support the allegation. The bottom line; were there found giants that support the claim -- human women did bear giants, with the fallen angels somehow responsible. Putting the time in perspective, when God created Adam and Eve about 4000BC, the fallen angels must have appeared much earlier but had been exceedingly sinful on earth between 4000BC and the flood around 2000BC.

> (Genesis 6:5-8) ⁵Then , the Lord saw that the wickedness of man was great in the earth and that every intent of the thoughts of _his heart was only evil continually_. ⁶And the _Lord was sorry that He had made man on the earth,_ and He was grieved in His heart. ⁷So the Lord said, "_I will destroy man whom I have created from the face of the earth, both man and beast, creeping thing and birds of the air, for I am sorry that I have made them._" ⁸_But Noah found grace in the eyes of the Lord._

God's response: destroying all but Noah and his family in the flood. Genesis 6 states that there would be giants after the flood. One can infer from the statement that "Giants also occurred after the flood" despite God's best intentions because the evil transferred with them. As we all know, wickedness is alive and well in our age, and we are about to repeat history as we approach the end of our time.

So, what other fallen angels' destructive actions caused God's angry response?

The phrase from

> Genesis 6:5 "that every intent of the thoughts of his (humanities) heart was only evil continually"

Genesis 6:5 covers it all. Through the fallen angels and their progeny, the Nephilim taught the women sorcery, incantations, and the divining of roots and trees, i.e., witchcraft. Since the Sumerian tablets pre-dated the Bible, their translated writings promoted the "God is an astronaut" theory. However, Christians know that the idea is not a fact.

As former Angels, fallen or not, one could assume, they were privy to many of heaven's secrets. They could have used that knowledge to do many amazing things, including genetically altering humanity to be part of man and animal. This assumption would account for the many strange images of the early Egyptian empires: part animal, human bodies with bird heads, etc. According to the C12 carbon dating method, tablets dated back to 5000 BC, but researchers never investigated associated ideological beliefs. So, several things are wrong with the Astronaut hypothesis. Since the Sumerians were the first to use writing, whoever initially transformed prior verbal scripture into the first cuneiform tablets could claim they were the scriptures' originators. However, since Satan is the great deceiver, his reputation and progeny's actions betray him. Godly Biblical stories passed on verbally from generation to generation could be known to everyone willing to listen: even before God cast out Satan. It would be only natural that one of his fallen angles cohorts, Enki, would take the truth of God and bend it to favor the Great Deceiver. He wrote the story of man's creation on fourteen tablets by plagiarizing the factual information from the ancient Biblical knowledge before God cast them down. Of course, he made himself a hero in the process. Notably, there was no acknowledgment that the flood was punishment for humanity's sinning, even though they admitted it occurred in the Sumerian narrative by Enki.

A study of different cultures identified the "Shining Ones" as "Angels of God." Other descriptions defined were "Watchers," which is also the meaning of the name Essen and "Sons of Light." Evidence shows the Essenes wrote the Dead Sea Scrolls that Biblical scripture accurately replicated in the Old Testament books.

It would be safe to conclude that these were the Godly representatives during this period. The scriptures and prophets created the Bible: not the Sumerian Cuneiform tablets. As Enki's story unfolds, it culminates in a nuclear disaster at the end of the age defined earlier. Earthlings are about to repeat the past and redo what happened generations ago in the first claimed extinction of man just before Adam and Eve. However, it is not clear that such an event occurred. Zecharia Sitchin further makes the following claim in The Lost Book of Enki.

Scholars and theologians alike now recognize the biblical tales of Adam and Eve's Creation, Garden of Eden, flood, and Tower of Babel texts written down millennia earlier in Mesopotamia, came from the Sumerians. They, in turn, explicitly stated that they obtained their knowledge of past events from a time before civilizations began, even before Mankind came to be, from the writings of the Anunnaki ("Those Who from Heaven to Earth Came")-the "gods" of antiquity.

While I agree that the tablets may have said these things, I would certainly deny that they were written or authorized by anyone resembling our Biblical God. In looking at their deeds, all of these actions belong to Satan. In this case, the truth is in the eye of the beholder. For nonbelievers in God and Jesus Christ, any excuse to claim we were created by "Gods" from outer space is better than believing the "truth." On the other hand, a Christian sees Satan's deceptive allusions that we are all Gods in training to do our own thing by invoking powers learned from the world's evil. It matters not to a nonbeliever that the pantheon of deities in that day was nothing more than a list of fallen angels (demons) raised to multiple Godly positions by Satan, contrary to the Biblical God.

# THE HERE

The interpretation of Here must be: NOW. What are the current conditions on earth we think will affect our salvation? This book started almost ten years ago. We are in the end-time, just before the return of Christ, meaning that the Antichrist will soon appear on the scene. The world is already starting to polarize itself to a path independent of God. The Antichrist is already beginning to do his thing: so, "who is he?"

## Satan's Role

*God has given Satan dominion of unbelievers only who, because of their disbelief, are blind to the glory of God."* How did this evil evolve on our earth? The books of Daniel, Revelations, Matthews, and numerous others tell the story.

Because Satan was in the Garden of Eden before he tempted Adam and Eve, *his first fall from God's grace occurred before God created man*. So why did our LORD throw Satan out of heaven this first time? H***e wanted to be God.***

Ezekiel 28:12-15 describes Satan as an exceedingly beautiful angel, probably the most admirable of God's creations; however, he was not content with his position. ***Instead,*** *Satan wanted to permanently "kick God off His throne since the Garden of Eden."* When God had thrown him down from heaven, Satan *still moved freely between heaven and earth,* retaining access to His throne, *speaking openly to God **in accounting for his activities.*** Notice the many prideful "I will" statements in the following:

> **(Isaiah 14:13-14):** [13] For you have said in your heart: '***I will ascend*** into heaven, ***I will exalt*** my throne above the stars of God; ***I will also sit on the mount*** of the congregation On the farthest sides of the north; [14] ***I will ascend above the heights*** of the clouds, ***I will be like the Most High.***'

**(Ezekiel 28:14-15):** [14]"You were the anointed cherub who covers; I established you; You were on the holy mountain of God; You walked back and forth in the midst of fiery stones. [15]You were perfect in your ways from the day you were created; Till iniquity was found in you.

**(Ezekiel 28:17).** "Your heart was [a] lifted up because of your beauty; You corrupted your wisdom for the sake of your splendor; I cast you to the ground, I laid you before kings, That they might gaze at you. *Satan, as ruler of the earth,* has blinded the nonbelievers from seeing or knowing anything about the glory of God:

**(2 Corinthians 4:4):** tells us that: "whose minds, **the god of this age** *(Satan)* **has blinded**, who do not believe, lest the light of the gospel of the glory of Christ, who is the image of God, should shine on them.

**(Job 1:6-7):** [6]Now there was a day when the sons of God came to present themselves before the LORD, and Satan also came among them. [7]And the LORD said to Satan, "From where do you come?" So Satan answered the LORD and said, "From going to and fro on the earth, and from walking back and forth on it.

Thus, from the above scripture, we know that while God threw Satan to earth, He still gave him visiting rights before His throne as an accuser to examine the loyalty of His disciples. The Almighty allowed Satan to test a righteous "Job" by removing all His blessings to see if he would remain loyal to Him. After showing that Job did not reject Him, God gave him everything before doubling in measure.

The authorship of the book of Job is uncertain. It is speculated to be written by Moses and claimed to be one of the oldest books in the Bible. Suffice it to say, someone wrote it before 100 AD, and we can compare it to when God wholly revoked Satan's trips before the throne. That day arrived on *September 23, 2017,* the fulfillment date of the Revelation 12 prophecy. On that date, war broke out in heaven. Michael and his angels fought and won against the dragon with his angels, so the great dragon, who deceives the whole world, was cast out: God disallowed Satan any further right to stand before Him from that day forward.

***Now we know why things have worsened in the years beyond 2017. It is because of the above date and an angry Satan.***

## Satan Thrown Out of Heaven

> (Revelation 12:7-12): [7] And war broke out in heaven: Michael and his angels fought with the dragon, and the dragon and his angels fought, [8] but they did not prevail, nor was a place found for them[1] in heaven any longer. [9] ***So the great dragon was cast out, that serpent of old called the Devil and Satan,*** *who deceives the whole world; he was cast to the earth, and his angels were cast out with him.* [10] Then I heard a loud voice saying in heaven, "Now salvation, and strength, and the kingdom of our God and the power of His Christ have come, for the accuser of our brethren, who accused them before our God day and night, has been cast down. [11] And they overcame him by the blood of the Lamb and by the word of their testimony, and *they did not love their lives to the death.*[12] Therefore rejoice, O heavens, and you who dwell in them! Woe to the inhabitants of the earth and the sea! ***For the devil has come down to you, having great wrath, because he knows that he has a short time.***"

Resulting from Michael's battle with Satan, God entirely revoked his ability to interact with Him. Knowing that his time is short, the devil's efforts will be focused on the earth until the Great Day of The LORD sweeps them away.

## Obama the President

The Tribulation will begin with a promise of peace from the Antichrist and church members departing God. The two scriptures that tell us are:

(Daniel 9:27) [27]Then he [comment: Antichrist] shall confirm a covenant with many for one week [comment: 7 years]; But in the middle of the week, He shall bring an end to sacrifice and offering. And on the wing of abominations shall be one who makes desolate, even until the consummation, which is determined, Is poured out on the desolate."

(2 Thessalonians 2:3-4) [3]Let no one deceive you by any means; for that Day [comment: return of Christ] will not come unless the falling away comes first, and the man of sin is revealed, the son of perdition, [4] who opposes and exalts himself above all that is called God or that is worshiped, so that he sits as God[c] in the temple of God, showing himself that he is God. (2)

While the person who becomes the Antichrist may not be aware of the process until it happens, he would have all the beastly attributes. But he may not yet possess the evil spirit giving him his supernatural powers. Therefore, in his cunning ruse, he will do his utmost to deceive the nations into believing he is the returned Christ.

Remember that Antiochus, Alexandra's brutal general who pillaged Israel and the Holy City in 164 BC, ***will be the model*** for the Godless Obama: the 2020+ Antichrist.

As president of the United States, all his actions were against God. When Obama signed the gay marriage law, the White House glowed with a rainbow around it as he mocked God by using His colors surrounding the Heavenly throne. The Bible will show signs and wonders from God to warn us of coming events. When Obama won the 2012 election, the winning lottery number in Illinois: was 666, the beast's mark. But, of course, you cannot find proof of it now because the far left would never allow that fact to appear again. His White House ungodly shenanigans showed who and what he was as a person; he was a homosexual married to a man posing as his wife, proven by pictures that showed a bulge in her dress that should not be there. Nothing he did ever reflected Christian values; he endorsed his lifestyle by being for abortion, gay marriages, and homosexuality, among other ungodly acts. One of his most egregious actions caught him red-handed in filing a long-form birth certificate that was forensically false.

And _unlike_ all the presidents before him, he openly disparaged the Biblical sermon on the mount. So, his legacy was utterly ungodly. Finally, and inadvertently he slipped into a hosted interview and said: The sweetest sound I know is the Muslim call to prayer. A top U.S. evangelical leader accused Sen. Barack Obama of deliberately distorting the Bible and taking a "fruitcake interpretation" of the U.S. Constitution."

There are several forms of lying to non-believers permitted under certain circumstances, the best-known being _taqiyya_ (the Shia name). These circumstances are typically those that advance the cause of Islam - in some cases, by gaining the trust of non-believers to draw out their vulnerability and defeat them. Obama uses all those techniques. In a prophetic statement on one of the Jim Bakker shows, Sadhu, a prophet of God, said that Israel would ultimately agree to partition their land for a Palestine State in a quid-pro-quo exchange for the Jewish Temple replacing the Dome of the Rock on the Temple Mount.

The UN continued annually to bring the vote to partition Israel to the council members. It resulted in the United States vetoing _**for 70 years**_ the Assembly's vote to partition: until Obama abstained, thus allowing the vote. Currently, 36 countries, mainly Muslim, do not recognize Israel. They contend that they are the rightful owners of that land and believe they should own all of Israel even though God gave that territory to the Jews in His covenant with Abraham. While God did not endorse the plan, He knew it would happen. Obama, refraining from the veto to not divide Israel, betrayed GOD's wishes and, _in the process, most likely identified him as the Antichrist_. He ignored the precedent of all previous U.S. presidents who vetoed any attempt to force Israel's partition over the last 70 years. Obama will pick up President Trump and Jared Kushner's well-intended treaty framework, modify it, and make it acceptable to the Arab world. Then, he would become the hero by changing the failed financial offering and making lemonade out of lemons by promoting a completed Peace Treaty agreeable with everyone **_until it turns into a lie_**. The timing could not be better. It would make Obama a shoo-in to become the next UN Secretary-General in 2022. Several prophetic ministries predict that the UN seat will be the emerging throne for the Antichrist– just in time to start WWlll: the Gog-Magog War. Obama will then be in the cat-bird-seat to push the NWO agenda that will end with him claiming, shortly after, to be the returned Christ.

A near-death experience experienced by a secular fifteen-year-old Jew in 2015 showed him of a coming war. When questioned by a church Rabbi, He commented: "So, Iran will join Obama, the UN - the whole UN. Yes, everyone, Russia, South Korea - the entire United Nations. Everyone. **_All 70 nations will rise against us._**

Also, recall earlier that in Daniel 9:26, scripture tells us that: And **_the people of the prince who is to come_** Shall destroy the city and the sanctuary.

Who were "the people" of the "prince who is to come?" Contrary to popular belief, they were not Europeans; the "people" were instead Muslim: i.e., Roman Troops conscripted from the surrounding Arab countries. Explicit in that observation, the Antichrist, "Prince," also must be Muslim. "Hope of Israel Ministries" gives us the following conclusion: overwhelming evidence from ancient historians defined the ethnicity of "Roman" people who destroyed Jerusalem and the Temple in 70AD as Muslims. Conscripted Roman soldiers came from the local populace of Arabs and Muslims that dominated the region that day. Syrians, Egyptians, and troops from Asia Minor made up the Roman legions of the Middle East. Thus, the Antichrist is Muslim.

One of the proofs submitted is from the book, Soldiers, Cities, and Civilians in Roman Syria (University of Michigan Press, December 21, 2000). Author Nigel Pollard, Ph.D., Professor of Roman History at Oxford University, examined the ethnicity, in detail, of the Roman eastern provinces' soldiers during the first century. After thoroughly reviewing the most recent scholarly writings on the subject, he became convinced the overwhelming majority of the soldiers who destroyed the Temple were primarily Syrians, Arabs, and Eastern ethnicity. An old reality emerged.

Jerusalem's and the Temple's destruction occurred because the soldiers disobeyed their commanders when ordered to quench the Temple fire. After all, their hatred of the Jews overwhelmed their fears of the generals.

*https://www.hope-of-israel.org/peopleofprince.html*

The people that God would so severely punish were the non-believers in Him and His Son, Jesus Christ. While the preceding verses point directly to Muslim countries where their people have harbored hate for Israel, the Jewish people, and Christians for centuries, we must also include the world population because of the hatred they share. Whether we like it or not, the fundamental question is, what happens if we do not love the **LORD** your God with all our heart?

## The Rebirth of Israel

## Israel becomes a Country

As we read and study Biblical prophecies concerning the last days, many signs around us strongly suggest we are approaching the return of Christ and the end of God's week. In "Prince of Darkness," Grant R. Jeffrey lists 38 fulfilled prophecies in our generation. However, he calculates the odds of accomplishing just six of these predictions, in one generation, as one in 15.6 billion; the odds of meeting all 38 are beyond comprehension.

However, Israel's rebirth cements all these things together and gives credence to the notion we genuinely are, witnessing an "end time" event. The fulfillment of Ezekiel and Isaiah's prophecy on May 14th, 1948, is essential to start the countdown. Without the existence of Israel, the presence of the other signs would mean little. The end-time events revolve around this small country, which seems to be always in the news. It is essential to understand that Israel's rebirth was a Biblical prophetic event: God had dispersed them worldwide to break His covenant in not obeying God's tenets by idol worshiping and not helping to spread the gospel. Without Israel, other future prophecies could not happen.

NASA_CMB_Timline

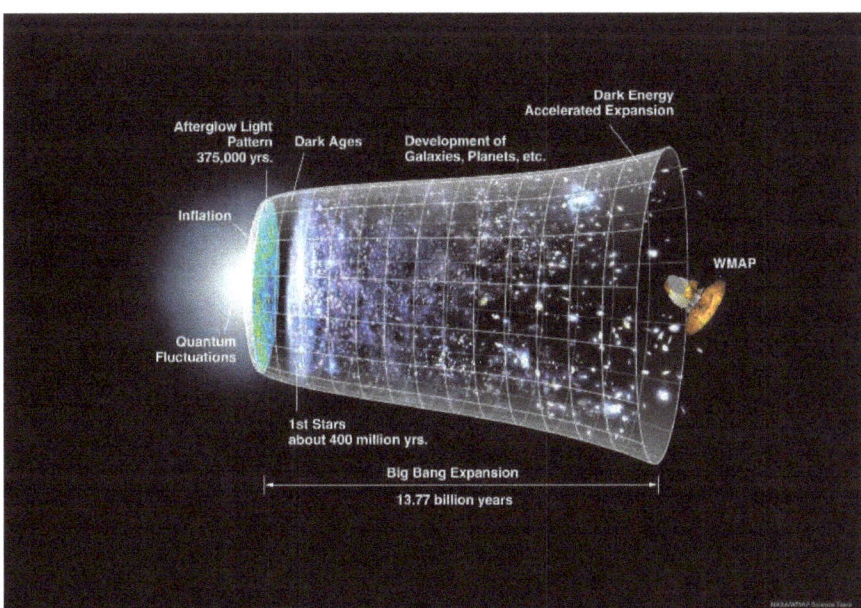

# Big Bang Theory

In the 1920s and 1930s, almost every prominent cosmologist proffered an eternal steady-state Universe theory. With the advent of scientists orbiting the Hubble telescope into space, humanity found that the universe was not static. The "Big Bang Theory" evolved using Alexander Friedman's governing equations to explain the new expanding universe. In 1929, Edwin Hubble discovered that distances to faraway galaxies were proportional to their redshifts, as Lemaitre initially suggested in 1927. His observation indicates that galaxies and clusters at enormous distances have an apparent velocity directly away from man's vantage point: the further away, the higher the apparent speed. Today, most world's cosmologists believe in the Big Bang Theory. Our universe began with an explosion of a singularity at a finite time in the past. It uniquely had infinite density and temperature.

The Bible had it right. Fundamental physics breaks down and knows little or nothing of events before. For instance, the example given in this book is that until the '50s, the most brilliant people in the world said the universe had always existed and was static. Guess what; they were wrong. The prevailing opinion is the "Big Bang" theory, which states that the universe began from nothing (a singularity), as the Bible has always said. That singularity was the "Word" of God, so The Bible is still ahead of scientific understanding. Humanity has not yet figured out or is afraid to admit the truth because it would be politically incorrect.

## Six days of creation?

The Big Bang Theory, coupled with Einstein's Theory of Relativity, can explain the disparity between the six days of creation and the universe's recognized age, approximately 13.7 billion years.

The Hubble telescope can see galaxies, supernovas, etc., and study these events in the furthest reaches of space, approaching as close as 380 million years to the big bang date. From these measurements, one can discern these far-off galaxies or supernovas' separation velocities and calculate the time separation between them.

In a study, physicist author Gerald Schroeder ("The Science of God" 1977) speculated that the previous expansions occurred faster than the latter. According to Einstein's theory of Relativity, Schroeder theorized that time is not constant in all situations. When the universe initially started from the "Big Bang," the fabric of space stretched at a rate near the velocity of light, thus causing instant inflation resulting in "time dilation." In this way, Schroeder hypothesized a new theory; that one can mathematically relate man's "billions of years" to God's six days of creation.

For instance: The first day would equal 8 billion years, the second 4, the third 2, the fourth 1, the fifth-day ½, and the sixth day ¼ billion years. The total for the six days would be 15.7 billion years -- close to the known age of the universe. Therefore, today's timeline would give the first six days of creation to take 15.7 billion years

Day 7's calculated 125 million years accounts for all the skeletons ever found that predated Adam and Eve. God created Adam in the Garden of Eden on the seventh day after the Neanderthals' age. In creating Adam and Eve, God did so in a paradise that promised mortality through the tree of Life. However, God initially made Adam and Eve Holy when He sanctified their creation. However, when they sinned and lost God's immortal gift, He posted cherubim at the east of Eden's garden to prevent regaining it by accessing the _tree of life_ against His will. They were not the same flesh and blood as the primitive Neanderthals, their forerunners. Only God can create life; why did He do it this way?

The evidence stemming from the previous analysis, if right, suggests God has gone through many iterations in bringing our human race to its present moment. It does not make sense to have an eternal God oversee humanity in our 7000-year age. Furthermore, Satan has controlled the 6-day week before GOD celebrates the Sabbath. Therefore, I would postulate that the data shows two distinctly different creations on Genesis days six and seven. Satan owns the six-day week. But, to offset what Satan will do in the first six days, God reserves the seventh day for people to worship Himself and His Son, Jesus Christ. There were two creations.

Moreover, mapping *the six days* of creation takes the first 13.7 billion years of the universe; using the same technique calculates day seven provides another 125 million years more than day six. That is too much evidence to ignore.

God's week throughout this book is composed of six days followed by a day of rest: the Sabbath. Satan controls the week and God the Sabbath. Why would not the above scripture follow the same six-day week protocol by identifying male and female as nonbelievers while the sanctified Sabbath identifies Adam and Eve on the seventh day as believers? If they were the same male and female, would He not sanctify the creation of the sixth and seventh day? Instead, he emulated the Sabbath, the seventh day, by additionally purifying it. As a result, he only blessed His creation on the sixth day.

God threw Lucifer and his angels down from heaven before Adam and Eve were in the Garden of Eden. These fallen angels had to have the ability to morph into flesh and blood to mate with earth women in delivering the so-called Nephilim – the early giants of the land. This earlier creation had all the attributes of the Devil -- there was no godliness.

Commenting on **Table 1**, in estimating the day value shown on page 67 of Schroeder's book, "The Science of God uses rounding of the calculated day one's 7.75 billion years, approximately an 8 billion value, as shown on page 60. This technique simplifies understanding the time for each day by rounding the calculated value to a simpler digit. Starting on day one after 8 billion years, day 2 follows with a 4-billion-year duration by halving day1, etc. Therefore, looking at Table 1 under the heading **"Start of the day**," using the same technique, the end of day 6 is .125 billion years, which also becomes the beginning of day seven, *not* included by Schroeder. The critical point is not the absolute accuracy but the exponential relationship linking closely to the universe's calculated age while still agreeing with the creation days. *Therefore, Schroeder's 15.75 billion years* did not yet include the time of the seventh day; i.e., the 125 million years I added now yields -*15.875 billion years, -- the new age of the universe*.

## COPYRIGHT PAGE

**Table 1 [Schroeder: day one through day 6; Talsoe day 7]**

| Day Number | Start of day | End of day | Cum God's week | Biblical Description |
|---|---|---|---|---|
| First | 8 billion years | 4 billion years | 8 bill | "Let there be light" – light appeared, called day. darkness appeared; called night |
| Second | 4 billion years | 2 billion years | 12 bill | He created firmament in the midst of the waters and called it Heaven |
| Third | 2 billion years | 1 billion years | 14 bill | God brought forth grass, yielding seed herbs, and fruit trees |
| Fourth | 1 billion years | .5 billion years | 15 bill | God created the Sun, Moon, and stars |
| Fifth | .5 billion years | .25 billion years | 15.5 bill | [21] So God created magnificent sea creatures and every living thing that moves, with which the waters abounded, according to their kind, and every winged bird according to its kind. |

| | | | | |
|---|---|---|---|---|
| Sixth Day | .25 billion years | .125 billion years | 15.75 bill | "Let Us make man in Our image, in the image of God He created him; ***male and female He created them***. God said to them, ***"Be fruitful and multiply***; fill the earth and subdue it; have dominion over the fish, birds, and every living thing that moves on the earth." (These beings would be the early prehistoric humans that pre-dated Adam and Eve) |
| Seventh Day | 125 million years | Current ~ 6000 years of an expected 7000 | 15.87 bill | On the seventh day, God ended His work that He had done, and He rested on the seventh day from all His work that He had done. *[comment: God must only have rested the first part of the seventh day because He created Adam and Eve after that. – we are now in the last part of the seventh day as I describe in this book." – very close to the end.]* |

The *estimated age* of the earth from a "Google search" is **4.543** billion years. From the new universe age of 15.875 billion years, subtracting the earth's age yields 11.33 billion years and coincides with day 2 of the Creation Calendar. This analysis indicates that the earth was in place after 11-12 billion years to allow day 3 and beyond. It further suggests that the planet's age (4.543 billion years) minus (the time of day **3 to 5** or **3.5 billion** years) would tell us how long it took to put the infrastructure in place to support life on day 6. Therefore, **4.543 –3.5 =~1.043** billion years ago, the earth was ready for humans on day 6. Subsequently,

*__1.043-.25__ [length of day 6 (in billions)] = .793 billion or ~__793 million years ago male and female appeared; (Genesis 1:26-28)__. Later, Adam and Eve arrived on the seventh day, which started ~__668 million years ago [793 million years - 125 million years]__. We are still in that last creation day when, around 4000 BC, God created Adam and Eve and have now advanced to six thousand years from their creation to our current calendar year of 2019: Again, "Time is short."*

These additional 125 million years range will embrace all old bones' dating, with the oldest being close to 3 million years, well within the 125-million-year bracket. This explanation indicates a definite correlation between the creation days and the earth's age. It also puts to rest the debate of the young-earth creationist theory that claims the universe, **Earth**, and all life were created by direct acts of God over a relatively short period, between 5,700 and 10,000 years ago. Under the above hypothesis, the Bible would have it right in stating it took six holy days plus one Blessed day to create Adam and Eve and the Universe. It did not say that we had to use God's calendar to translate the time rather than our own. While there is no earthly logic to justify two separate creation days, "__27__ _So God created man in His own image; in the image of God_ **He created him; male and female He created them.** Compared to: the _Lord God_ **formed man of the dust of the ground, and breathed into his nostrils the breath of life;** _and man became a living being._ The only reason I could believe God did it this way is that He had sanctified the 7th day as holy and would want to create His spiritual progeny on that Holy day.

## WERE ADAM AND EVE THE FIRST HUMANS?

Over time, humanity has wondered why *Paleoanthropologists* found so many skeletons dating back millions of years, predating the estimated creation date of ~4000 BC for Adam and Eve. In addition, human DNA contains between 1-10% of Neanderthal DNA, clearly showing that people existed and mated before Adam and Eve.

If one expected Adam and Eve to be the first people, a _close reading_ of (**Genesis 1&2**) suggests something different. In reading these passages, one easily can miss God's choice of words in defining His creations:

**(Genesis 1:27-31**) <u>On the weekday.</u>

<sup>27</sup>So God created man in His own image; in the image of God He created him; *male and female He created them*. <sup>28</sup>Then God *blessed* [Comment: *Look favorably on]* *them.* <sup>31</sup>So the evening and the morning were **the sixth day**.

Note that God [made alive] male and female: He *[spoke to them]* and *blessed* them. So this *man and woman* were *alive* before Adam and Eve. Who were they?

**(Genesis 2:3,7) *On the Sabbath.***

<sup>3</sup>Then God *blessed* [Comment: *Look favorably on*] the **seventh day** and *sanctified* [Comment: made free from sin, i.e., Holy], <sup>7</sup>And the Lord God formed man of the dust of the ground, and breathed into his nostrils the breath of life; and man became a living being.

Note: God only *blessed the* weekday, whereas He both *blessed and sanctified* the Sabbath. The definition of the keyword in each scripture, *blessed* is *an adjective* that describes something, while *sanctified*, [being made Holy] *is a verb*. The first Male and female creations were probably the Neanderthals that predated Adam and Eve. They were blessed because of the creation moment, whereas in the second creation, it was not only blessed but also sanctified, made holy, thus differentiating between believers and unbelievers,

An adjective has no power to change. Therefore, compared to the Sanctified, the first creation being merely blessed are unbelievers while the *sanctified*, Holy, Adam and Eve are believers.

The above viewpoint shows that Adam and Eve were Holy until they ate the forbidden fruit. The calculated period gives plenty of extra time to account for all the skeletons ever found that predated Adam and Eve. God created Adam in the Garden of Eden on the seventh day after the Neanderthals' age. In creating Adam and Eve, God did so by making them immortal in the Garden of Eden paradise before they fell. However, they did not remain immortal after the fall. To ensure they remained mortal, God posted cherubim at the east of Eden's garden to prevent their access to the tree of life. They were the first flesh and blood to become mortal by eating the forbidden tree's fruit. They were not the same flesh and blood as the primitive Neanderthals, their forerunners. Only God can create life; why did He do it this way?

### Beast from the Sea

As the future unfolds, we are about to enter the tribulation, where we soon will find out who the Antichrist is. Nonetheless, few will believe it. The beast has always been here with its hate for Jews and Christians – it has just grown and matured.

> (Revelation 13:1-9) Then I stood on the sand of the sea. And I saw a beast rising up out of the sea, having seven heads _[comment:7 kingdoms]_ and ten horns, _[Comment: Horns are 10 kings that arise out of "this beast kingdom."]_ **_and on his horns ten crowns, [comment: for ten uncommitted nations]_** and on his heads a blasphemous name. ² Now the beast which I saw was like a _leopard_, [Comment: represents Greece – 4 generals] his feet were as the feet of a bear [Comment: Iran/Persia], and his mouth like the mouth of a lion [Comment: Babylonia]. **The dragon gave him his power, his throne, and great authority.**
>
> ³And _I saw one of his heads as if it had been mortally wounded, and his deadly wound was healed._ And all the world marveled and followed the beast. **⁴_So they worshiped the dragon who gave authority to the beast;_** and they worshiped the beast, saying, "Who _is_ like the beast? Who can make war with him?" ⁵ And he was given a mouth speaking great things and blasphemies, **and he was given authority to continue for forty-two months** [Comment: 3.5 years]. ⁶Then he opened his

mouth in blasphemy against God, to blaspheme His name, His tabernacle, and those who dwell in heaven. **⁷It was granted to him to make war with the saints and to overcome them.** [Comment: WWIII, Gog—Magog war]. And authority was given him [Comment: Antichrist] over every tribe, tongue, and nation. **⁸_All who dwell on the earth will worship him,_** whose names **_have not been written_** in the Book of Life of the Lamb slain from the foundation of the world. ⁹ If anyone has an ear, let him hear.

Before the Ottoman Realm, the Roman Empire was the one to devour all the rest and had both a western and a mid-eastern leg. The remnant of the west portion is presumed to be the Euro-centric collection of nations gathered around a single currency. As the 1683 (Image 6) map shows, the Ottoman Empire consumed the Mid-East leg of the Roman Empire that had shifted its capital from Rome to Constantinople: renamed Istanbul. Amazingly, Istanbul, the Roman and Ottoman Empire capital, is shaped like a little horn: Aptly named the Golden Horn.

The Beast *will be* the _seventh head_ alluded to as the "little horn" -- the Antichrist, yet to come (Daniel 8:8-10). It had come and gone without people realizing it was here or had left. From the beginning of Egypt until the 1923 end of the Ottoman Empire, there was an unbroken line of Empires or Heads ruling the Middle East. The beast's seven heads represent seven united kingdoms or empires; therefore, if one head is mortally wounded, the whole beast dies. The beast **_you saw_** was the Original Ottoman Empire symbolized by the Leopard representing Turkey and its allies. Losing WW1, Germany caused the Ottoman Empire to fragment into separate countries, thus killing the beast.

_Turkey is the remaining nation_ **trying to bring a neo-Ottoman Empire back to life** _by restructuring the Caliphate._ **However, it will ascend out of the bottomless pit and go to the abyss, becoming the 8th beast when it reconnects with the ten yet uncommitted Muslim nations who will again form the neo-Ottoman Caliphate,** becoming the end-times "**is:**" **Satan.** Virtually all of the countries surrounding Israel are

Islamic and thus had absorbed Rome's remnant Eastern leg. Interestingly, today, August 28, 2014, Turkey announced a new Caliphate Federation as an umbrella for all Islamic nations as I am writing this.

The spiritual head of the Sunni Muslim world recently declared they would establish the Caliphate in Istanbul: i.e. the little Horn (Golden Horn) prophesied in the Bible. Turkey would provide a center for all these Muslim states, asserting, "This is the destiny of Turkey." The confederation would combine (Wahhabis) Sunnis, and Persian (Shiites), suggesting they should resolve their differences with a plea to reject the terrorism of radical Muslims. Recep Tayyip Erdogan, the new Turkish President, accepted credit for pushing Turkey in this new direction.

*Chicago: The Future Muslim Caliphate, Confederacy In Turkey.., https:// www.youtube.com/watch?v=bp7v2svathQ (accessed March 10, 2019).*

Analysis of Daniel's image in Dan 2 suggests that the kingdom would be like a mixture of Iron and clay that would not adhere to each other. "Arab" in Hebrew means "a mixture." Daniel further alludes to being mixed by saying: "*They will mingle with the seed of men, but they will not adhere to one another*," i.e., mixed -- being Arab *[Comment: will not assimilate into other cultures]*. Turkey was the seat of the Ottoman Empire, but it was also the seat of the Eastern Roman Empire when Rome moved its Capital to Constantinople.

> (Ecclesiastes **1:9**) says it all: ⁹ That which has been *is* what will be, That which *is* done is what will be done, And *there is* nothing new under the sun:
>
> Matthew 24 describes a *massive tribulation that no one had ever seen before,* which has not yet happened in our lifetime. It thereby rejects thoughts that the earlier ***Antiochus IV's*** abomination might have been that event.

Furthermore, Jesus, in Matthew 24, was telling about a future evil because His discussion talking to His disciples was 200 years after Antiochus's discretion. The given interpretations in

(Daniel 8:17,19,26) from Gabriel state: ¹⁷ Understand, son of man, that the vision refers to the time of the end," ¹⁹ for at the appointed time the end shall be ²⁶ Therefore seal up the vision, for it refers to many days in the future."

All the above can only mean it is for the last day of the age. Daniel 8 and 11 is a parallel scripture to Ezekiel 38-39. They establish templates of what to expect in the future by showing what happened in the past. Syria, as King of the North, is just north of Israel. The new beast country's designation as "far north" acknowledges the location is further north than its predecessor: i.e., Syria to be replaced by Turkey and its allies as the new King of the North.

The story of how all this happens follows: At the peak of his power, Alexander died a premature death becoming the "broken horn," resulting in his replacement by four less powerful horns, generals, from the old Grecian Empire: *(i.e., **Greece, Turkey, Syria, and Egypt**)*. Of the four, **Turkey,** *the Little Horn,* would become Satan and overcome *Greece, Syria, and Egypt* in forming the combined **neo-Ottoman Empire** Caliphate of the dragon**.**

Metaphorically foretelling what would come in the future follows as we look toward the end of time.

(Daniel 8:9-12) ⁹And out of one of them came a little horn [Turkey] which grew exceedingly great toward the south [Egypt], toward the east, [Persia/Iran] and toward the Glorious Land [Israel]. ¹⁰And it grew up to the host of heaven [Satan/Antichrist]; it cast down [Challenges God] some of the host and some of the stars to the ground, and trampled them. ¹¹He [Satan/Antichrist] even exalted himself as high as the Prince of the host [Comment: Christ] and by him, the daily sacrifices were taken away, and the place of [f]His sanctuary was cast down. ¹²Because of transgression, an army was given over to the horn [Neo Ottoman Empire with 10 Islamic nations] to oppose the daily sacrifices; and he cast truth

down to the ground. He did all this and prospered: i.e.,
The 7-year reign of the Antichrist.

Christ identified this little horn as Satan's seat, thus designating Satan's throne in _Turkey from where he would give authority to the False Prophet and the Antichrist._ The beast would become the Ottoman Empire, thus ending the Eastern Roman Realm from contention. Moreover, Turkey's selection also would eliminate Europe or the United States for that honor. Finally, with its allies, Turkey would become the northern king in Ezekiel 38 and 39, who will fight God in the Gog-Magog war following the Antichrist's taking of Israel: WWIII.

One should note that several scriptures defining the beast are Daniel 7, 8, and Revelation 13, 17. They are consistent and offer different details that are clues in establishing the beast's identity.

The Beast's formation history traces back to Alexander the Great's death. After his death, the empire was divided into the northern part, going to Alexander's generals, **Seleucid, Antiochus IV,** who received **Babylonia** and much of Alexander's eastern provinces. **At its height of power**, the Seleucid Empire included central **Anatolia, Persia,** the **Levant,** and **Mesopotamia**.

Modern-day names for these countries are:

- Anatolia, **(Modern Turkey)**
- Persia, **(Iran)**
- Levant **Cyprus, Hatay, Israel, Jordan, Lebanon, Palestine, and Syria**
- Mesopotamia **(Babylonia, "now Kuwait"), Afghanistan, Turkmenistan, northwestern parts of India, and Pakistan.**

Daniels' prophesied wars between the north and south kings followed the Grecian Empire break-up after Alexander's death. Antiochus was one of a string of monarchs that played their part over time in the Seleucid dynasty as the king of the North. He reigned from Antioch in Syria, whereas the **South's king** received the southern half of the territory, i.e.,

Egypt, and ruled from Alexandria. The King of the South used ***Ptolemy,*** the secular version of the dynasty name.

Before analyzing the beast's symbology, we should note the differences between the beast identified ***from the sea*** and ***the earth***. The sea consists of metaphors correlating a nation with a particular animal. Nations are Empires. The creature from the sea evolved from empires, where the succeeding nation absorbed and replaced its predecessor. Revelation places the beast in our emerging future. It has a ***leopard*** body that identifies itself as the most recent beast, the Ottoman Empire, by its other body parts. Although the monster, *in part, is an Empire or a Kingdom,* it also interchangeably identifies with *the Satanic organization that guides it: the dragon (Satan), the Antichrist, and the False Prophet.* It is the triune Christian antithesis consisting of God, Jesus Christ, and the Holy Spirit. *As its political leader, the Antichrist would speak for this kingdom,* allowing him to curse God and worship the dragon.

The above beast describes both attributes of a nation or empire and human qualities that imply it gives interchangeability between its beastly characteristics and those of its political leader. Following is his nasty delegation of power:

The sequence of empires taken from TIME MAPS

https://www.timemaps.com/history/middle-east-1500bc/

> (Revelation 17:8-14) [8] The beast that you saw was, and is not, and will ascend out of the bottomless pit and go to perdition. And those who dwell on the earth will marvel, whose names are not written in the Book of Life from the foundation of the world, when they see the beast that was and is not, and yet is.[10] There are: (a). Also, seven kings. (b) Five have fallen, (c) one is, and the other has not yet come. (d) And when he comes, he must continue a short time. 11 The beast that was, and is not, is himself also the eighth, and is of the seven, and is going to [f] perdition. [12] "The ten horns which you saw are ten kings

who have received no kingdom as yet, but they receive authority for one hour as kings with the beast. [13] These are of one mind, and they will give their power and authority to the beast. [14] These will make war with the Lamb, and the Lamb will overcome them, for He is Lord of lords and King of kings; and those who are with Him are called, chosen, and faithful." The listed dates showed when that empire defeated its predecessor in the number sequence.

The above shows that Satan has not changed his stripes – although the various countries may have changed their name over time, they are predominantly Muslim. That is not to say one can paint the country with a broad brush by inferring there are no Christians in each of them; God calls to all of us. However, where there are many Radical Islamists, Christians and Jews will be persecuted by those who hate them.

DANIEL 11

To reach a particular level of evil, we would have to wait for a prior Grecian General named Antiochus IV Epiphanes to inherit the Levant territory to become the King of Syria after Alexander the Great died. Antiochus became the Antichrist model that the Bible would use to echo his Abomination of Desolation arriving in our future:

Antiochus IV Epiphanes was the notorious King of the North in Daniel 11, performing the previous desecration of the Jewish Temple in 167 BC. His clashes with Egypt occurred roughly in 330 -164 BCE.

The following Daniel 11:1-39 scripture presents a narrative that paraphrases the battles between "Syria," the King of the North, and "Egypt," the King of "South," which evolved into the Northern King's persecution of Jerusalem

> (Daniel 11:36-39)[36] "Then the king [Comment: Antiochus] shall do according to his own will: he shall exalt and magnify himself above every God, shall speak blasphemies against the God of gods, and shall prosper till the wrath has been accomplished; for

what has been determined shall be done [Comment: persecution of the Jews]. [37]He shall regard neither the [q] God of his fathers nor the desire of women, nor regard any god; for he shall exalt himself above them all. [38]But in their place he shall honor a god of fortresses [Comment: Zeus]; and a god which his fathers did not know he shall honor with gold and silver [Comment: Idol worship], with precious stones and pleasant things. [39]Thus, he shall act against the strongest fortresses with a foreign god [Comment: Zeus], which he shall acknowledge, and advance its glory; and he shall cause them to rule over many, and divide the land [Coment: Israel] for [r]gain.

## OT North and South Kingly Battles

(Daniel 8:23) [23] "And in the latter time of their kingdom, When the transgressors have reached their fullness, _A king shall arise, Having fierce [a]features, Who understands sinister schemes._

(Daniel 11:31) [31]And [a]forces shall be mustered by him, and _they shall defile the sanctuary fortress; then they shall take away the daily sacrifices, and place there **the abomination of desolation**._

The Ptolemy Kingdom's _first_ battle with Antiochos IV started in 170 BCE because of Egypt's demands for returning their claimed property, i.e., Coele-Syria. Antiochos preemptively attacked Egypt, concerned with their dispute, capturing King Ptolemy and all his territory except Alexandria, which remained under siege. Antiochus hoped to avoid upsetting Rome by allowing the Egyptian King, Ptolemy VI (his younger brother), to continue ruling as a puppet monarch under his control. Feeling he now controlled Egypt, Antiochus withdrew _his attack_ on Alexandria and headed home. Meanwhile, Alexandria's councils no longer threatened but decided to _select a new king named_ Ptolemy (VIII

Euergetes). To avoid civil war, Alexandria's leaders strategically chose to jointly rule with the original king, his younger brother (Ptolemy VI).

Antiochus, now no longer in charge of Egypt, never lost his intent of recovering control. In 168 BC, he led a second attack to reclaim Alexandria, with the broader goal of *adding ships to capture Cyprus*. However, before reaching Alexandria, he was blocked by a Roman counsel with a Senate message to immediately cease the battle by withdrawing his armies or face war with Rome. Antiochus complied.

Thus, Antiochus, enraged by losing control over his puppet king and further thwarted by Rome, denying him the right to re-attack Alexandria, attacked Israel instead. Verses 36-39 of Daniel 11 describe Antiochus's pillaging and devastation of Israel/Jerusalem in verses 40-45 before his plan to head back to Syria. Having a natural hatred of the Jews following their Covenant with God, he outlawed the faithful's religious rites and traditions by ordering them to worship *Zeus* as the supreme god (2 Maccabees 6:1–12). This desecrating act of sacrificing a pig on Zeus's altar in the Holy Place of the Jewish Temple resulted in the Biblical term "Abomination of desolation," where people were told they must worship the idol of Zeus or die. Because the Jews refused to obey, Antiochus severely persecuted them by sending an army to enforce his decree. They slaughtered many and destroyed Jerusalem because of their resistance. Antiochus's persecution of the Jews in Jerusalem was between 168 to 167 BC. The following verses, 40-45, imply one thing, *but the reality is something else. Scholars claim that the above verses are historically correct, but there is a mystery in the last five scriptures: 40-45.*

## NT New King of the North

> **(Daniel 11:40-45)** **⁴⁰ "At the time of the end"** the **king of the South shall attack him;** and the king of the North, shall come against him like a **whirlwind, with chariots, horsemen, and with many ships**; [Comment: metaphors for weapons of war] and he shall enter the countries, overwhelm them, and pass through. **⁴¹** He shall also enter the Glorious Land [Israel], and

many countries shall be overthrown; but these shall escape from his hand: Edom, Moab, and the [s]prominent people of Ammon [all in Jordan]. **42** He shall stretch out his hand against the countries, and the land of **Egypt** shall not escape. **43** He shall have power over the treasures of gold and silver, and over all the precious things of Egypt; also, the **Libyans and Ethiopians** shall follow at his heels. **44** But news from the east and the north shall trouble him; therefore, he shall go out with great fury to destroy and annihilate many. **45** **And he shall plant the tents of his palace between the seas and the glorious holy mountain, yet he shall come to his end, and no one will help him.**

# DISCREPANCIES IN DAN 11:45-50

The supernatural event occurs when Daniel 11:40 starts **_explicitly_** with: **_"At the time of the end."_** That phrase appears _only once_ in the Bible: it describes a leap from Antiochus's BC time into the 2020+ future where the end days' final time will become the new day, **_"At the time of the end_**" when the Lord returns on 2020+?. Antiochus would become the foreshadowing archetype of our future Antichrist yet to come.

The phrase **_time of the end_** refers to the period immediately preceding the _last day_, **_"At the time of the end._** It supports the specific time of verse 40 in Daniel 8:17, 11:35, 11:40, 12:4, and 12:9, referring to this end-time vision, when the growth of understanding must happen, finally ending by saying knowledge will increase and to close the books and seal the words till **_the time of the end: i.e., the final day._**

There can be no misunderstanding that we are at **_the end of God's week_**, especially when the last verse tells us: "_Go your way, Daniel, because the words are rolled up and sealed until **the time of the end.**_

Contrary to history, verses 40-45 infer another third war between Egypt and the King of the North would occur: it did not. Further, the last verse, 11:45, says: **_he shall_** [future tense] **_plant the tents of his palace between the seas_** [Mediterranean Sea] **_and the glorious holy mountain, yet he shall_** [future tense] **_come to his end, and no one will help him._**

When battling the Antichrist and his army, this last sentence suggests God traps him between the Mediterranean and the Dead Sea, where he kills him.

> (Dan 11:45) And he shall **_plant the tents of his palace between the seas and the glorious holy mountain;_** yet he shall come to his end, and no one will help him.

(Joel 2:20) "But I will remove far from you the northern army, And will drive him away into a barren and desolate land, With his *face toward the eastern sea, [Sea of Galilee], And his back toward the western sea;* and its stench will come up, And his foul odor will rise Because he has done [1]monstrous things."

God had trapped the Antichrist's army between the Mediterranean and the Sea of Galilee, 60 miles from Meggido, the site of Armageddon.

That army had grown from the early Syrian Beast to a neo-Ottoman Empire Caliphate that picked up ten Muslim nations in acquiring its size. It became the new King of the North, formerly the beastly name for Antiochus, in 168 BC. It became known as Gog-Magog or interchangeably the neo-Ottoman Empire.

Had we believed the war between the King of the north and Egypt took place in 168BCE, Antiochus would have died in Judea battling the Jews. Instead, history tells us Antiochus perished in a campaign against the emerging Parthian Empire, with Persia providing him his grave. Since Antiochus did not die in Judea, verses 40-45 reflect the *future*. So it would be Daniel's end-time event *yet to come* and placed in *the oncoming years of 2020 and beyond?* This monster will be the new grown-up beast described earlier, born out of the *Ottoman Empire and* killed by being on the wrong side in WW1. It would be grown from 10 uncommitted countries' promises to support the neo-Ottoman Caliphate in the upcoming battle with Christ at Armageddon.

(Zechariah 12:2-3): [2]"Behold, I will make Jerusalem a cup of drunkenness to all the surrounding peoples when they lay siege against Judah and Jerusalem. [3]And it shall happen that day that I will make Jerusalem a burdensome stone for all peoples; all who would heave it away will surely be cut in pieces, though all nations of the earth are gathered against it.

(Revelation 2:12-13) [12] "And to the [f]angel of the church in Pergamum Turkey write, 'These things says He who has the sharp two-edged sword: [13] "I know your works, and where you dwell, where Satan's throne is. And you hold fast to My name and did not deny My faith even in the days in which Antipas was My faithful martyr, who was killed among you, where Satan dwells.

Again, this interpretation tells us the beast would come from the Roman Empire's Mid-east leg, indicating **he will be Islamic**. Joel Richardson notes that all the previously questioned identities reside in Turkey, the latest beast country.

(Luke 21:20): warns us [20] "But when you see Jerusalem surrounded by armies, then know that it's *[comment: Abomination of ]* desolation is near.

The fourth Ashen Horse of Seal 4 accounts for killing 25% of the earth's population for all reasons, i.e., by the sword, with hunger, death, and the earth's beasts suggest war. The killing of close to 1.9 billion people *just before* mid-tribulation would indicate the beginning of the battle for Jerusalem.

# DISCOVERY OF THE ARK OF THE COVENANT

The most important thing to list over that period is Ron Wyatt's discovery of the Ark of the Covenant, the dead sea crossing Noah's arc, and the site of Sodom and Gomorrah. Ron had prayed to God to let him lead someone to heaven. Ron Wyatt executed extensive excavations in the Garden Tomb area for approximately ten years, beginning in January 1979. Then, at two in the afternoon of January 6, 1982, Ron Wyatt broke into a cave beneath the Calvary escarpment north of Jerusalem's city wall. It contained the Ark of the Covenant, the table of shewbread, and several other items not seen because of animal skins, boards, and stones covering them.

God used Ron to wonderfully discover the Ark of the Covenant, Noah's Ark, and the Exodus crossing point of the Red Sea. When Ron first became aware of Christ and believed that He had died for him, promising eternal life on request, he made such requests repeatably. "LORD, I want to be saved," he said. I want to be in heaven with my family. He expected things would change, but they did not. Like many of us who have the best intentions to do right, the world gets in the way, and we never get around to it. Frustration happens. In Ron's case, he followed up by praying that God would lay a burden, for souls, on his heart that he could not resist. He prayed to the LORD to help him find something to lead someone to heaven. God answered Ron's prayer many times over.

**Ron Wyatt Discoveries**

While sightseeing near his hotel by the Damascus Gate, Ron walked along an ancient stone quarry, known as "the Calvary Escarpment, not far from the garden tomb. He began a conversation with a local authority that unexpectedly turned out to be the head of the Department of Antiquities in Jerusalem. As they strolled in the garden area, they began discussing Roman relics, and Ron told him of his discovery of Noah's Ark and his theories of how the Pyramids came to be. Then, in a magical moment, Ron stopped walking, and his *left arm, with a mind of its own, suddenly pointed to a bunch of rubble* that had been there for hundreds of years. *Next, his voice involuntarily said, that's Jeremiah's grotto, -- the Ark of the Covenant is down there.* He realized he had never thought of finding the Ark of the Covenant – he had not even ever researched it. His new friend walking with him asked, what did you say? I think that's Jeremiah's Grotto, and the Ark of the Covenant is down there. His Antiquities friend said you should dig there, and we will give you a permit to excavate and a place to stay, have your laundry done, and furnish your meals. However, Ron's conservative nature prompted him to say: I have to go home and look up the scriptures and ensure this is possible. Ron thanked him and stated that he would come back after returning to the United States. Fortunately, Ron and his sons were in Jerusalem because Ron had gotten severely sunburned from diving for chariot parts in the Red Sea, and they were only back to await their plane home.

Ron knew that he had a supernatural event with his arm pointing and his voice telling him that the Ark of the Covenant was where he pointed. Unfortunately, the research did not mention the Ark beyond Jeremiah – it was never mentioned again until Hebrews 9 and Revelation 19 near the end of the Bible. This lack of recognition occurred when the Babylonians started the war that led to Israel's 70-year captivity. Therefore, he believed it was still in Jerusalem. Ron surmised that the Priests had hidden the Ark somewhere near the edge of the city before the army destroyed it because there was no indication in scripture that they took it as part of the loot from the Jewish Temple that made its way to Babylon. Therefore, he presumed it was between Babylon's siege and Jerusalem's walls.

While the following apocryphal literature is not in the Biblical canons, it is a part of the religious history that rings true concerning how the Ark of the Covenant found its way to its present resting place.

## Hiding the Ark

## Jeremiah Hides the Tent of the LORD's Presence

> 2 Maccabees 2:4-8 [4]These duplicate records also tell us that Jeremiah, acting under divine guidance, commanded the Tent of the LORD's Presence and the Covenant Box to follow him to the mountain where Moses had looked down on the land which God had promised our people. [5]When Jeremiah got to the mountain, he found a vast cave, and there he hid the Tent of the LORD's Presence, the Covenant Box, and the altar of incense. Then he sealed up the entrance.
>
> [6]Some of Jeremiah's friends tried to follow him and mark the way, but they could not find the cave. [7]When Jeremiah learned what they had done, he reprimanded them, saying, _No one must know about this place until God gathers his people together again and shows them mercy._ [8]_At that time he will reveal where these things are hidden, and the dazzling light of his presence will be seen in the cloud, as it was in the time of Moses and on the occasion when Solomon prayed that the Temple might be dedicated in holy splendor._

## The crucifixion site

The Romans selected the execution site close to the most highly traveled route north, outside the city wall. Most everyone between Jaffa, Jericho, Damascus, and Natal would pass and see the executions. This road would have been natural because routes to the South, East, and the West, crisscrossed by large gullies, made travel self-limiting because the terrain was too steep.

How does this description agree with the Bible? Gospel writers call the site of Jesus's crucifixion _Golgotha_ derived from an Aramaic word meaning "the skull." Calvary is the Latin form of the name. While Scripture does not reveal the precise location of Golgotha, causing some debate, it merely states that Jesus' crucifixion took place *outside* the city of Jerusalem, though near it. The fact that passers-by mocked Him indicated it was a well-traveled road agreeing with Ron Wyatt's description of his discovered site.

> Matthew 27:39 [39] And those who passed by blasphemed Him, wagging their heads.

The Romans cut out three recessed areas into the rock base that would hold signs describing the person under crucifixion and their crime. According to the Bible, in Christ's case, His crime said: Jesus, the King of the Jews. Of the three holes in front of Christ, two were for the robbers crucified on either side of Jesus.

> (Matthew 27:37). [37] And they put up over His head the accusation written against Him: THIS IS JESUS THE KING OF THE JEWS.

The only other strong candidate for the possible crucifixion site is The Church of the Holy Sepulcher, just outside the walls but south and west of Ron's discovery. A long-time traditional view held by the Roman Catholic, Greek Orthodox, Armenian Orthodox, and to a lesser degree, the Egyptian Copts, Syrian Christians, and Ethiopians is that the church was the location of the crucifixion and burial of Christ. Protestant beliefs regarding Christ's crucifixion aligned closer to Ron's targeted digging area near the Garden Tomb and The Place of the Skull, north of the wall. Ron began digging in this location along an escarpment in the Garden Tomb grounds, where he previously spoke his involuntary words and pointed with his left hand. It was at a spot about halfway between the Garden Tomb and the Place of the Skull.

The initial excavation attempts began, in 1978, at Ron's pointed area. That place contained an enormous boulder barely exposed above the surface, inducing Ron to dig several yards to the right. It was a job of mammoth proportions where Ron and his sons would remove tons of rock and debris while sifting through it all for any artifacts. This search was a requirement of the Department of Antiquities that always demanded compliance.

In proceeding to dig straight down, they noticed shelf-like niches cut into the face of the cliff. After further searching, they saw three slots with a smaller one on the right side. Ron immediately believed that these places would be where the signs describing the crucified victims' crime were in three languages: Greek, Hebrew, and Latin. The warning, explaining the victims' offense, would have to appear in plain sight of the passers-by to be a deterrent.

While digging 30 feet down through the soil along the escarpment, Ron uncovered four crucifixion holes,12x13x23 inches deep, in solid rock, one on a higher level and about ten feet out from the bluff. He found three more on a lower level, four feet below and further away from the cliff. Jesus Christ had the single, higher cross-hole designated for the chief person in the group of three.

## The Ark Found

A beautiful garden next to the crucifixion site is north of Jerusalem's city wall. In that Garden, less than 200 feet from the place of Jesus's crucifixion, His chiseled-out tomb is on the face of the cliff. In his earlier trips, when he first found the Ark of the Covenant, he discovered that the stone box's lid had been broken and rotated, exposing the mercy seat. There were only about eighteen inches of clearance between the ceiling and the debris covering the artifacts below. Shining his flashlight through the massive pile of large stones, he caught a glimpse of something shiny. Dry-rotted timbers with rotted remains of animal skins just beneath the rocks hid the artifacts below from view. The animal skins covered a gold veneered table with a raised molding around the side consisting of an alternating pattern of a bell and a pomegranate. It was the Table of Shewbread. Next, Ron, with adrenaline flowing, looked to see what else was visible. Shining his light on the ceiling, he spotted a crack with a dark substance and slowly and painfully crawled over the rocks to the rear of the chamber, where he saw a stone case extending through the stones. He knew the Ark was in the stone case whose cover had broken in half. One end of the stone cover had slid to its side, showing dry blood on both edges of the broken lid. Above the Ark, the crack in the ceiling was directly over the top's split opening, allowing the dark substance to fall from the roof crack into the stone case's split cover.

Ron realized what happened in this serendipitous moment: Christ's blood had found its way to the Mercy Seat of the Ark of the Covenant hidden inside this cave in 567 BC. God had arranged 600 years before the birth of Christ that His son's blood would reach the Mercy Seat upon His crucifixion. This miraculous event ratified both the Old and the New Covenant and fulfilled Daniel's 9:24 prophecy to "Anoint [with Jesus's blood] the Most Holy [The Ark of the Covenant]. Then, with an earthquake, God had opened a crack from the base of the cross some eighteen to twenty feet above the Ark to allow Christ's blood and water to flow from His ruptured spleen to the Mercy Seat. Aftershocks then sealed the hole so that subsequent water from storms over the years would not contaminate the site.

Ron noted that crucifixions typically did not involve a lot of blood, but in this case, the centurion stuck a spear in Christ's side to ensure He was dead. Thus, this crucifixion was bloody: copious amounts of blood and water gushed out from Christ's side. In addition, Ron moved around on his back or stomach on earlier trips because of the confined space. Thus, during his first three visits, the images were either "washed out" or blurred when taking pictures with different cameras.

In another miracle, everything had changed; he discovered that the cave holding the Ark of the Covenant had become clean. All the debris was gone. Somebody had done what he expected: clear and haul all the rubble away. In the cleaned-out cave were four young men that turned out to be angels. One of them said they had been guarding the Ark ever since Moses had put the tablets of stone in the Ark. The furnishings all sat in perfect order. The Ark of the Covenant was sitting against the wall at the end of the cave. It was 12 feet long and 18-foot high, and the wall appeared to be of beautiful crystal that radiated the colors of the rainbow as it is, in heaven, over the throne of God. It also seemed to serve as the light source for the chamber. The shewbread table, the candlestick, and the golden altar of incense were all spread out in the earthly temple. The angels lifted the Mercy Seat, and Ron, in wonder, estimated the

Mercy Seat, being of solid gold, weighed about 900 pounds. The stone tablets were in the Ark of the Covenant, and Ron removed them with the four angels' assistance at their request. The angels told Ron that God wanted everyone to see them, and they are now available to show when the proper time comes.

Ron handed the tablets to the angel, who put them on a stone shelf near the original entrance used in hiding the Ark over 2500 years before. *The angel then told Ron they would be shown with the blood when the Beast law's mark was passed and in force.* The "Beast Law" is presumed when the Sunday law gives Sunday *the only day of worship for all religions.* This human-made law will require that you break God's ten commandments. Nothing much had changed since Christ's days on earth when he had told the Pharisees in Matthew 15:9, **9**and in vain, they worship Me, teaching *as* doctrines the commandments of men. You will receive the beast's mark if you keep those human-made laws and break God's ten commandants.

**_God's display of His evidence will be brought forth by a person of His choosing to be seen by the world_**. This Ark videotape, recorded by Ron Wyatt, will be scientific evidence showing God's eternal law written with His finger in stone. Jesus' blood, having a chromosome count of 24, spilled upon the mercy seat of the Ark, undeniably proves He is the Son of God. *This irrefutable proof will be God's show-and-tell witness to the world of His Son's sacrifice for lost humanity.*

> (Psalm 89:34) <sup>34</sup> My covenant I will not break, Nor alter the word that has gone out of My lips.

God tells us He will not break His contract with us or modify the things He has spoken in delivering His law, the Ten Commandments written in stone on the mountaintop. If you keep that law, you will receive the seal of God. *Soon there will be a set of human-made legislation aimed at creating a one-world government with a one-world religion as prophesied in the book of Revelation in the Bible, where all who comply will receive the beast's mark.*

## Christ's Blood

Acting on one of the angels' requests, Ron scraped some dried blood from the sides and lid of the cover for chromosome analysis. Since dried blood is dead, Ron asked the Lab people in Israel to perform their investigation; they told him that while they could get DNA and some other information, they could not get a chromosome count unless the blood was alive and well. However, they planned to reconstitute the blood in a saline solution for 72 hours at body temperature with a slight, gentle, swirling motion. Ron stated he wanted to be there when they checked it out. They said okay. When he arrived to see the results, they indicated human blood. Ron asked them to take some white blood cells, put them in a growth medium, and keep them at body temperature for 48 hours. The Lab techs said that would do no good because the blood was dead. Ron asked them to please humor him and do it. The techs acquiesced, and in that growth medium, it became white, living blood cells. Doing what Ron requested, the blood came alive, and within 48 hours, it gave a _chromosome count of 24_. After chattering among themselves in Jewish for a short period, they asked: Where did you get this blood? Whose blood is it? _Ron, weepily, said: it is the blood of your Messiah. This blood is unique; it is the blood of Jesus Christ._ Ron also said: I assure you those men's lives have changed.

The information about Christ's blood proving He was God's Son is particularly noteworthy. His chromosome count was 24, 23 from the mother, and one "y" from the father, indicating it was not human but _from God_. People have 46, 23 from the father and 23 from the mother. 22 of the 23 autosome pairs are typical for both males and females. The 23rd pair for an average woman is Xx, and the male is Xy. Christ's chromosome count of 24 means that he got all the physical traits from his mother's 23 because only a single added y chromosome would give 24. _This blood conclusively proves that it came from a virgin birth._

**Ron Wyatt's Conclusion**

What I would like every man, woman, and child in this audience to remember, if you forget everything else, is Jesus Christ, the Son of the Living God, in full cooperation with his father, loved us to the point that they were willing to give His son's life on our behalf. It's done, folks; we have been bought with the price, but it will do us no good unless we go to the Father in the name and blood of his son and ask for forgiveness and restoration to his likeness. As you can see, I'm a relatively old man; there have been some experiences that I've encountered along the way, some helpful, some educational, and some leaving scars behind. But one important lesson I learned when I first became aware of Christ and believed He had died for me; He said that eternal life was available upon request. Well, I made that request repeatedly, LORD: I want to be saved, I want to be in heaven, and I want my mom, dad, brothers, sisters, and my old grandma to be there also. I prayed those prayers, and my life didn't change a bit. It was a list; I did what Paul said he had done. I knew I shouldn't do it, but I did it. Things I wanted to do, good stuff -- never got around to it. I couldn't manage it somehow or the other, so I asked the LORD to help me out of this horrible mess. I was impressed to request that he lay a burden for souls on my heart that I could not resist. I started praying for that. He did it, and he loves everybody all over this earth. *If He wants me to go around and share his incredible artifacts and words of light, and He helped me do it, I'll keep at it. When I started praying that God would change me and do whatever was necessary to allow Him to work in and through me to help others to be saved, things began to change.* That's what I recommend that you do, folks.

*You should ask the Father in the name and blood of his Son to come into your life through the power of His Holy Spirit, forgive you, cleanse you, help you to quit sinning, and help you to reflect His character to the point that people are attracted to Him by your influence.* When I get to heaven, I'm going to look around, and I want to see everyone there. You can make it with God's help. Christ is here tonight. He says where two or three are gathered together in my name; I am there in the midst of them. Please, take advantage of this fantastic opportunity.

Authenticity

I offer the following statement from his site for those doubting the authenticity of what Ron has discovered.

http://www.arkdiscovery.com/gruver.htm

**Henry Gruver's Testimony about the testing of Christ's blood:**

Around 1990 in Phoenix, Arizona, at the Full Gospel Business Men's Fellowship (FGBMF), Southwest Regional Convention, I was at the table when Demos Shakarian, founder of the FGBMF. Demos had assembled a special meeting with Ron Wyatt. In addition, an attorney and a document specialist were present. The meeting's purpose was to validate the certificates he had received from the laboratories, proving the samples' authenticity taken from his discoveries. Ron had a blue, three-ring binder containing those certificates in plastic document protectors. It included certificates from six labs – three in the USA, one in Jerusalem, one in Germany, and other declarations of his lab testing.

One of the lab result certificates pertained to the chromosomes of the dried blood Ron discovered in the cave beneath the cross holes that had flowed down onto the Ark of the Covenant. Another lab result pertained to Ron's discovery of Noah's ark. It confirmed that the specimen was, in fact, a piece of "petrified, laminated wood" with "resins" in-between, which are "presently unknown to man."

When Ron opened his blue, three-ring binder, the document specialist asked permission to remove their plastic folders' certificates. Ron reluctantly granted permission to remove them from the document protectors, as long as he didn't tamper with the documents or perform ink tests on the signatures. The man removed them from the plastic and looked at each certificate carefully. He had a giant, thick book, eight by eleven inches and about six inches wide. In it, he had brought the names and data for all the labs in the countries where Ron had lab tests done. In his book, he could look up each lab, record numbers, and compare all the signatures with the ones on the certificates. Thus, he was able to validate the record numbers from each document. As a jeweler would do, his technique looked at each signature with a magnifying glass. When he finished scrutinizing each one, he said, "I would verify the authenticity of these documents to the top court in this land." And he was a registered document specialist in the nation at that time.

## SHROUD OF TURIN - Proof of Resurrection

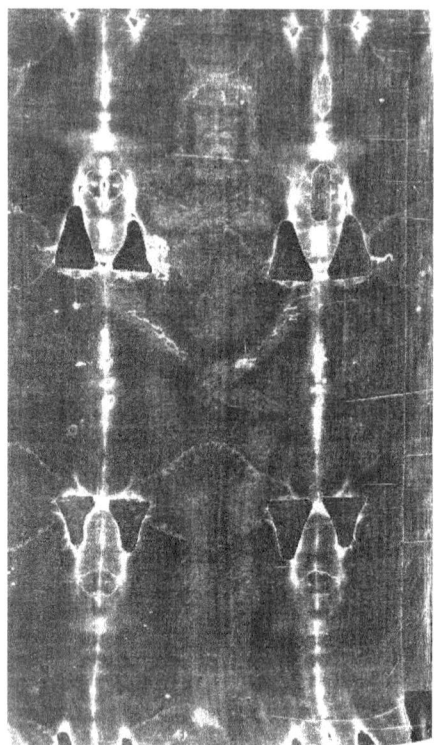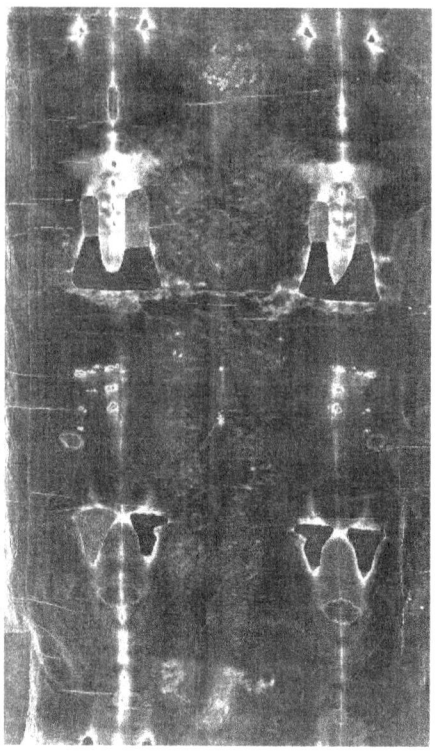

The Shroud of Turin uses its Biblically correct entire front and back image to validate Jesus Christ's resurrection. The cloth proves the existence of God with flawlessly aligned evidence. Fully aligned front and back photos could only come from the resurrection energy between the sheets. The underlying question is: why do some people disbelieve the evidence?

While believers do not need proof because of their faith, the following evidence may impress unbelievers. The Shroud of Turin is the alleged burial shroud of Christ. An extended cover wrapped the body, head to toe, starting at the feet and going up, around the head, and back down to the feet. It displays a body image on both the top and bottom sheets that accurately registers between the two and shows all the trauma of a crucifixion consistent with the Biblical description of what Christ endured. The shroud images are essential "negatives" of the body that, when photographed, display a "positive" photo; Just as in photography

A particle physicist has said that an indeterminate energy source between the two sheets had to have manifested and taken the picture to create the perfect image top to bottom. While not knowing what that energy source was, the physicist stated it had to have happened? In my opinion, the image resulted from radiation energy variations caused by spacing changes between the sheets and the body. It led to the scorched discoloration profile on the shroud. The covering to the figure's closest parts provided the darkest appearance, like an ordinary negative used in photography. As in photography, the shroud's taken image reverses the blackest spots giving the "x-ray" looking image that shows the facial features—this all 2000+ years before anyone knew anything about photography. In a supporting experiment, Dr. Accetta injected a radioactive solution typically used in x-ray procedures into his veins. www.shroud.com/dallasmt.htm.

Conclusion: An emitting radiation model can best explain some essential Shroud image characteristics. No other human model study has approximated the Shroud image this faithfully." The account states the "radiation" from the veins, holding the hot fluid in the body when scanned outside the body gives a similar effect seen on the Shroud Turin without as much detail. However, the cumulative effect was far from emulating the Shroud's image. The scientific explanation for the "Life-Giving" radiation is unknown.

©1978 Barrie M. Schwortz Collection, STERA, Inc.

On top of that, there was 3D information that allowed sophisticated software to create a full-body image. In contrast, in any other 2D model, constructing a 3D image from 2D details resulted in severe distortion. In my opinion, shared by many others, that power source was the burst of life coming from the resurrection of Christ while enclosed by the shroud. A set of secret laws of physics, yet unknown to science, exists. Furthermore, the study proved that no paint pigment was involved in creating the image. The threads' staining showed only a millionth of an inch penetration, causing investigators to presume it was an x-ray-like emission that caused radiation scorch. Using that analysis, the Shroud itself entirely validates the Bible.

In a paper by (Williams) Peter S.Williams, "The Shroud of Turin: **A Cumulative Case for Authenticity,"** he summarizes this excellent treatise. It states:

The Shroud is perhaps the most intensely investigated artifact of history. It has come under the scrutiny of many scholars and researchers, including historians, archeologists, chemists, physicists, botanists, engineers, doctors, forensic pathologists, and experts in painting, photography, textiles, philosophy theology, and philosophy theology apologetics.

First photographed in 1898, the image was analogous to a negative similar to today's photographic process. However, filming the shroud resulted in a positive impression that looks like the description of Christ at the crucifixion. The claim is that now some scientists believe in its authenticity more readily than medieval Christians do.

Flawed early "carbon dating," indicating that it was a fraud, resulted from a poor decision in cutting a sample from a fire-damaged corner of the Shroud. Subsequent investigation has shown that the cloth does date back to the time of Christ. Furthermore, an artist, to fake the Shroud, would have had to do some of the following improbable tasks:

### Shroud of Turin - face image

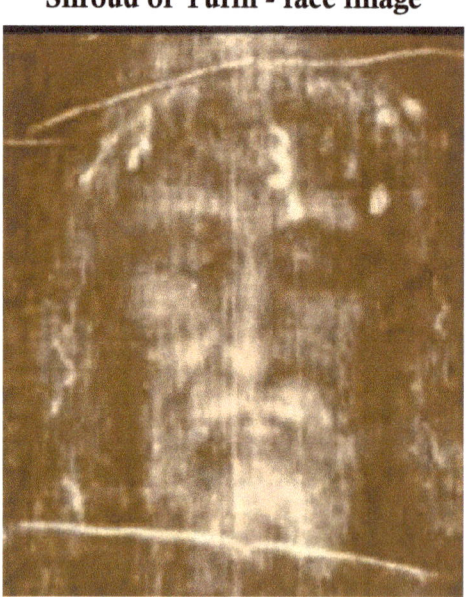

## Requirements for Fake replication

1. Find a 1st-century burial cloth from Jerusalem with the correct weave.
2. Paint an anatomically perfect human using a level of medical knowledge otherwise unknown in the fourteenth century. This data is consistent with the burial of Jesus as described in the gospels
3. Paint the body in a photographically negative manner, centuries before the invention of photography.
4. Use a 1st-century burial cloth from Jerusalem or obtain and 'salt' a suitable fabric (with the proper 1st-century weave) with pollen from just the right flowers
5. Paint blood flows in perfect forensic agreement with death by crucifixion
6. Do so using rare blood from the limited AB group with a significant amount of bilirubin.

## Other Proofs

7. There was no sign of brush strokes or paint pigment.
8. The image created on top of the blood on the shroud showed that it happened postmortem.
9. Observations of the atomic blast at Hiroshima showed photographic shadow images left on building walls of people killed in the explosion, similar to the shroud's image.
10. The shroud's blood showed 22 autosomes plus 1 Xx chromosome from the mother with only one male Y, equaling 24 total, indicating a virgin birth.
11. A burst of energy from a short wavelength laser gave similar staining to the Shroud.
12. 3D information, coded into the image, allows software generation of a hologram from 2D details that otherwise, in any other case, would result in severe distortion.

In summary, the complete data, when statistically evaluated, shows the probability of fraud for the Shroud was one chance in 82,944,000—converting (1-1/82994000) to percent yields a (99.99999879%) likelihood that it was the burial shroud of Christ; --- about as close as one could get to 100. Hence, the presented data convincingly predicts that the Shroud of Turin covered the Son of God. Therefore, it validates the presence and resurrection of Jesus Christ, and, truthfully, the Bible is the word of God.

## AKIANE

### God teaches Alaine to paint

Occasionally God gives humanity a gift as a child prodigy that can show the wonders of His Glory. Such a gift is Akiane Kramarik, who at age four told her mother, "God is teaching me to paint." Besides that, God was out to make a point because both Akiane's parents were atheists. As atheists, the parents, initially, never talked about religion, never prayed together, and did not attend church. So Akiane's first sharing of her vision with her mother came out as:

"Today, I met God," Akiane whispered to me one morning.

Her mother thought: "What is God?" I was surprised to hear this; God's name always sounded absurd and primitive.

"God is light – warm and good." "it tells everything and talks with me. It is my parent."

Asked to tell more about her dream, her answer:

"It was not a dream. It was real." (pg7 – 63words)

At four, Akiane began sketching hundreds of figures and portraits. Her house became her easel with drawings covering the white walls using fireplace charcoal or stains from fruits or vegetables to be her equivalent paints.

One day her parents noticed white stains on her front teeth. Akiane's brother tattled by saying:

"Akiane ate a tube of toothpaste." When her mother asked, "why," the answer came back, "because her Angel's teeth were so white they sparkled, and Akiane wanted her teeth to get just as white." She then drew a sketch of her angel, who accompanied her during her Heavenly visits. (pg9 – 49 words)

At the age of eight, Akiane wanted to paint a portrait of Christ and looked long for a model but could find no one. Finally, in frustration, she asked her parents to pray with her throughout the day for a "model," telling God that she could not find anyone by herself. She prayed:

"I need you to send me the right model and give me the right idea. Maybe it is too much to ask, but could you send him right through our front door: "Yes, right through our front door." In the middle of the afternoon, the very next day, an acquaintance brought her friend, a carpenter, right through the front door. She introduced him to Akiane, thinking the young artist would like his features. Standing almost seven feet tall, the carpenter had strong hands and a warm smile. Tai jis!: This is He Akiane blushed.

Akiane said this is whom I have seen in my visions. But a week later, the carpenter called her to apologize, stating that he felt unworthy to represent his Master and had to decline the honor. Akiane refused to give up, praying more feverishly that day, the next day, and the next. Another week had passed before the carpenter called us back. "God wants me to do it." (pg 26-27 –163 words)

## JUDGING THE PAINTING-SHROUD EVIDENCE

When superimposed over the Shroud of Turin photo, the incredible picture of Christ, made by Akiane at eight years old, shows a perfect virtual match. The trickle of blood over the Christ image's left eye on the Shroud superimposes in the same place over the left eye of Akiane's painting. What are the odds a picture by 8-year-old Akiane would be such a close match to a photo from the 2000+-year-old shroud? She knew what He looked like from her trips to Heaven; then had the incredible experience of God delivering the model to her door in answer to her prayers. Furthermore, in yet more overwhelming proof, Colton Burpo, the subject of the book "Heaven is for Real," selected this image that looked like the Jesus he saw on his visit to heaven.

For a disbeliever wanting scientific proof that there is a God, the closest thing to direct evidence is the Shroud of Turin. A logical principle

(Occam's razor) attributed to the medieval philosopher, William of Occam, states that one should not make more assumptions than the minimum needed to solve the problem. It underlies all scientific modeling theory and admonishes us, describing a given phenomenon, to choose the simplest model from a set of otherwise similar ones. Occam's razor principle eliminates superfluous variables or theories not needed to explain any given model results. Using this most straightforward method, the statistical probability of failure is minimal. Summarizing the below important events, strengthening the argument for the presence of God and Jesus Christ is the following:

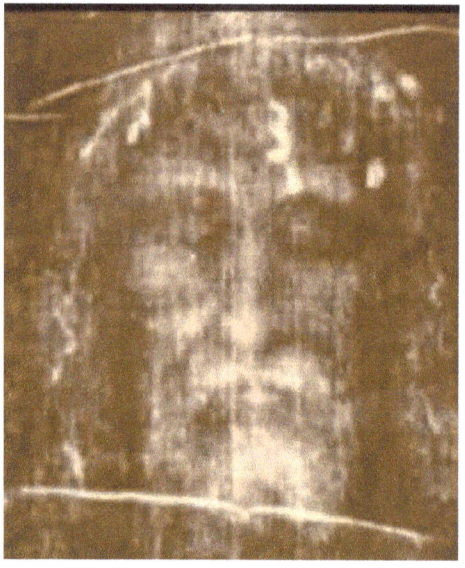

- Occam's razor principle, applied to the Shroud of Turin, would state; that the resurrection, life-giving energy, centered in the body of Jesus between the sheets caused the perfectly non-painted image on the Shroud. It is the simplest explanation.

- **As previously stated: In assessing the Shroud, some scientific conclusions** indicate that they believe the Shroud did cover the body of Christ. A calculated probability that it covered the body of Christ was (99.99999879%), or conversely, only one chance in 82,944,000 that it was a fake.

- Akiane Kramarik (an eight-year-old prodigy artist and daughter of an atheist father and mother) painted a Christ portrait, where she claimed her teacher was God; it closely matches the Shroud image.

- The Akiane painting of Christ, identified by Colton (Burpo, 2010) from the book Heaven is for Real," is the remembered face of our Lord seen in his Heavenly visit.

Comparing that painting to a photo of the Shroud's face by superimposing the picture over the shroud's face using computer software shows an almost perfect match. What is the probability of such a portrait being an ideal match to the photo from the shroud? – Answer: somewhere between slim and none. Couple this equivalent with Colton Burpo's statement that Akiane's "Prince of Peace" painting was the Christ he saw in Heaven, the same one remembered by artist Akiane during her heavenly art lessons. The entire image described by this combination of events is a miracle presented by God as proof seen by our eyes. Faced with this circumstantial evidence, how can one not believe that God and Jesus Christ exist and now reside in Heaven? Is the compelling evidence enough to convince the skeptics to ask: How do I make sure I am "born again" and "Ready?"

# THE HEREAFTER

"Hereafter," as a noun, means *Life after death*.

The Lord had told me that the correct rapture-tribulation timeline was as important as the ten commandments. If not correctly interpreted, His followers would not understand what is ahead in the final days. So, the key to untangling Daniel 9:27 is to analyze the Scripture's nuances, so everyone realizes the massive implication of their impact.

> Daniel 9:27
>
> Then he, [Antichrist], shall confirm a covenant with many for one week:

- i.e., *seven* years. Implied to be a peace treaty between Israel and the surrounding Islamic countries
- But in the *middle* of the week
- This comment identifies two consecutive 3.5-year periods compose the seven-year tribulation.
- He shall bring an end to sacrifice and offering.
- The implication is that the Antichrist has captured Israel and the Holy City and thus terminated the earlier allowed sacrifice and offerings.
- And on the wing of abominations shall be one who makes desolate, Even until the consummation, which is determined, Is poured out on the [1]desolate."
- The interpretation of a covenant as seven years shows that it will include all humanity: no exception, no pre-trib or post-trib.

Other Scripture will show that the first 3.5 years is the Wrath of the Lamb while the last 3.5 years will be the Wrath of God. At this point, the Scripture defines an image that shows the Wrath of the Lamb on the left-hand side, accounting for the first 3.5 years, with the *Wrath of God* representing the last 3.5. This analysis infers that Satan emerges during the first half of the seven years and will rule the final half.

The *Wrath of the Lamb,* controlled by Christ, will explain all the Revelation 6 Seal punishments. Then, through His angels, God will handle the Trumpet and Bowl judgments with His Wrath as they did during Exodus.

Occasional readers unfamiliar with Daniel's Timeline's numbering system will have difficulty understanding it. However, within the seven years, the Rapture/Tribulation narrative tells its story by following the chronological events from the start of the tribulation to its Armageddon end.

In scripture, 3.5 years often appears in days, months, i.e., as an example:

| | |
|---|---|
| 42mo/12 mo./yr. | = 3.5 Year. |
| 1 month | = 30 days (prophetic year). |
| [times, times and a half time], | = 3.5 Year |

Therefore, time in the evolving graph image may show months or days to reflect 3.5 years. Jesus taking the "elect" to heaven happens after the first half of tribulation, i.e., at the seven-year mid-point. Mattew 24's Olivet Discourse will explain and give the best overview of what is coming next. The future image will increase from two rudimentary consecutive 3.5-year periods to the taking of saved souls to heaven at Mid-trib.

## Matthew 24 (Olivet Discourse)

*The end-time* is those seven years of trouble we have never seen before, culminating with our saviors' return. Christians have anticipated this moment for over 2000 years, with nonfulfilled dates sprinkled throughout that period, so why, after all that time, should we expect His return is imminent?

The two dreams stating that "Time is Short" and a request to write this book with its given title, God the HERE and the HEREAFTER, are reason enough for me. When I started to write, I had no idea what *short* meant. Scripture may not provide us with the time and the date, but as we shall see, it shows us the season. I found Matthew's Olivet Discourse delivers the best overview of what is coming. Many parallel scriptures will agree with it and provide greater understanding. Since it covers much of what is next, the complete Scripture is for future reference.

Matthew 24:1-50

Jesus Predicts the Destruction of the Temple

²⁴Then Jesus went out and departed from the Temple, and His disciples came up to show Him the buildings of the Temple. ² And Jesus said to them, "*Do you not see all these things? Assuredly, I say to you, not one stone shall be left here upon another, that shall not be thrown down.*"

The Signs of the Times and the End of the Age

³Now, as He sat on the Mount of Olives, the disciples came to Him privately, saying, "*Tell us, when will these things be? And what will be the sign of Your coming, and of the end of the age?*"

⁴And Jesus answered and said to them: "*Take heed that no one deceives you. ⁵For many will come in My name, saying, 'I am the Christ,' and will deceive many. ⁶And you will hear of wars and rumors of wars. See that you are not troubled; for [a]all these things must come to pass, but the end is not yet. ⁷For nation will rise against nation, and kingdom against kingdom. And there will be famines, pestilences, and earthquakes in various places. ⁸All these are the beginning of sorrows.*

⁹ *"Then they will deliver [*future tense*] you up to tribulation and kill you, and you will be hated by all nations for My name's sake. ¹⁰And then many will be offended, will betray one another, and will hate one another. ¹¹Then many false prophets will rise up and deceive many. ¹²And because lawlessness will abound, the love of many will grow cold. ¹³But he who endures to the end shall be saved. ¹⁴And this gospel of the kingdom will be preached in all the world as a witness to all the nations, and then the* end will come.

## The Great Tribulation

[15]"Therefore when you see the 'abomination of desolation,' spoken of by Daniel the prophet, standing in the holy place" (whoever reads, let him understand), [16] "then let those who are in Judea flee to the mountains. [17] Let him who is on the housetop not go down to take anything out of his house. [18] And let him who is in the field not go back to get his clothes. [19] But woe to those who are pregnant and to those who are nursing babies in those days! [20] And pray that your flight may not be in winter or on the Sabbath. [21]For then there will be great tribulation, such as has not been since the beginning of the world until this time, no, nor ever shall be.

[22]And unless those days were shortened, no flesh would be saved; but for the [c] elect's sake those days will be shortened.

[23] "Then if anyone says to you, 'Look, here *is* the Christ' or 'There!' do not believe *it*. [24]For false christs and false prophets will rise and show great signs and wonders to deceive, if possible, even the elect. [25]See, I have told you beforehand.

[26] "Therefore if they say to you, 'Look, He is in the desert!' do not go out; *or* 'Look, *He is* in the inner rooms!' do not believe *it*. [27] For as the lightning comes from the east and flashes to the west, so also will the coming of the Son of Man be. [28] For wherever the carcass is, there the eagles will be gathered together.

## The Coming of the Son of Man

[29]"Immediately after the tribulation of those days the sun will be darkened, and the moon will not give its light; the stars will fall from heaven, and the powers of the heavens will be shaken. [30] Then the sign of the Son of Man will

appear in heaven, and then all the tribes of the earth will mourn, and they will see the Son of Man coming on the clouds of heaven with power and great glory. [31] And He will send His angels with a great sound of a trumpet, and they will gather together His [d]elect from the four winds, from one end of heaven to the other.

The Parable of the Fig Tree

[32]"Now learn this parable from the fig tree: When its branch has already become tender and puts forth leaves, you know that summer *is* near. [33] So you also, when you see all these things, know that [e]it is near—at the doors! [34] Assuredly, I say to you, this generation will by no means pass away till all these things take place. [35]Heaven and earth will pass away, but My words will by no means pass away.

No One Knows the Day or Hour

[36]"But of that day and hour no one knows, not even the angels of [f]heaven, but My Father only. [37]But as the days of Noah were, so also will the coming of the Son of Man be. [38] For as in the days before the flood, they were eating and drinking, marrying and giving in marriage, until the day that Noah entered the ark, [39] and did not know until the flood came and took them all away, so also will the coming of the Son of Man be. [40] Then two *men* will be in the field: one will be taken and the other left. [41] Two *women will be* grinding at the mill: one will be taken and the other left. [42] Watch therefore, for you do not know what [g]hour your Lord is coming.

Only Matthew 24:22 will account for the Rapture change. *The length of the saint's tribulation will shorten to 3.5 years by rapturing them before the last 3.5 years,* thus disallowing them from participating in the *Antichrist's* entire seven years. _Shortened days_ explicitly state **_all flesh will be subject to the tribulation, thus placing_** all punishment within the 7-years boundaries:

Analysis of the above is validated by;

(Daniel 7:25) "25….Then the **_saints shall be given into his hand For a time and times and half a time [comment: 3.5 years],_**

_This period_ could only be the first 3.5 years _within the seven-year boundaries: not pre or post-tribulation._ The _saved_ of the whole population will receive their punishment in those first years. Thus, it validates the Scripture saying the saints would only be in the Antichrists' hands for 3.5 years. After that, Satan's left behind will move forward into their punishment days of the Great Tribulation.

### Tribulation Overview

**_Daniel 9:27_** 's Antichrist is the proverbial wolf in sheep's clothing. The wolf disguises himself as a sheep by wearing a slaughtered coat and enters the flock to capture a meal: the Antichrist in search of souls appropriately fits the bill. He is the seed that begins the end-time story that delivers the stark level of God's punishment on the wicked while protecting His followers from the same fate.

The following scripture will tell us that the rebuilt temple must exist in our end-time to allow the Jews to sacrifice and worship: this has not yet happened, nor has the Antichrist given us his seven-year peace covenant. Therefore, rebuilding must be a high priority if we are close to entering the tribulation. Daniel 9/27 is happening because we are at the end of God's 6000-year week under Satan's rules. As the Sabbath for the week, Christ's 1000-year reign will follow in the wake of Armageddon, So God's _total age_ is 7000 years. Aside from the above, the following scriptures tell us nothing is new under the sun. God, to no avail, also has warned us in the past. Humanity always did its thing: they ate, partied, drank, married, etc., ignoring God's warnings. The Bible tells us that those who do not belong to Christ will analogously suffer the pangs of a woman giving birth. They begin slowly but become exponentially worse; the delivery will be the Lake of fire for the unrepentant.

> (2 Peter 3:8) But, beloved, do not forget this one thing, that with the Lord *one day is as a thousand years* and *a thousand years as one day*: ergo, God's week is 6000 years

> (Revelation 11:2) ²But leave out the court which is outside the Temple, and do not measure it, **_for it has been given to the Gentiles. And they will tread the holy city underfoot for forty-two months_**.

i.e., the Antichrist will own the Temple Mount for 42 months. As my *red board vision* said: Time is short. The churches should tell their congregations, "do you know that Christ will be coming in your children's lifetime? The proof is simple. Scripture tells us: Some believers see the hint of what is coming, but unfortunately, few have tried to interpret Revelation's intimidating read. As a result, they are unaware of the punishments humanity will receive, nor the massive earth changes that will wipe out most of society. As in Sodom and Gomorrah and Noah's time: we will likewise suffer the unfolding prophecies in the book of Revelation.

> (Luke 17:26-30) ²⁶ And as it was in the days of Noah, so it will be also in the days of the Son of Man: ²⁷ They ate, they drank, they married wives, they were given in marriage, until the day that Noah entered the ark, and the flood came and destroyed them all. ²⁸ Likewise as it was also in the days of Lot: They ate, they drank, they bought, they sold, they planted, they built; ²⁹ but on the day that Lot went out of Sodom it rained fire and brimstone from heaven and destroyed *them* all. ³⁰ Even so will it be in the day when the Son of Man is revealed.

> (1 Thessalonians 5:3) alludes to the painful tribulation by noting: "While people are saying, 'There is peace and security,' then sudden destruction will come upon them

as labor pains come upon a pregnant woman, and they
will not escape."

The birth pangs of a woman in labor aptly describe the 7-year tribulation:
i.e., tolerable pain at the beginning followed by unimaginable agony in
delivery.

Modern-day visions from prophetic ministries have "Born Again"
Christians *raptured* immediately after the first nuclear event on U.S. soil.
Its ramification will hugely affect the world and leave a giant vacuum for
loved ones left behind. But, on the other hand, it will cause a massive
revival as humanity absorbs all the happenings and realizes God is
real. Many will turn to Him, who will protect them while on earth,
and if circumstances result in martyrdom, He will keep them from fear.
Nonetheless, the Bible tells us that none of us are without sin.

We have entered the seven-year tribulation, where we will all receive
punishment for our sinfulness. At the start of this trial, with the
manifestation of the prophesied Covid-19 virus, one more indicator
of the end-times: Matthew 24:7, *there will be pestilence*. While future
reprimands will come our way, GOD will treat His Christian followers
far better than those who do not believe. If you confess your sins, repent
and ask for forgiveness, and ask Christ to guide you forever, you will
become "born again" and ensure your ticket to Heaven. Even as a remnant
"left behind" survivor, you may still receive salvation if you accept Christ
during the Great Tribulation. GOD.'s Seal on your forehead will protect
you from His wrath.

An unrelenting stream of punishments will befall the unbelievers as the
Tribulation unfolds. This period is called The Great Tribulation. The last
3.5 years of the 7-year sentence will bring in the prophecized end-of-
the-age events preceding Christ's return. It will lead to Armageddon and
initiate His millennial reign. Finally, the last question: how close are we
to that end date – and can we know?

Based on my dream, God wants me to give a *"time is short"* message
regarding the return of Christ. Emphasizing the point, I repeatedly

found the exact phrase in my research. While we may not know the precise hour, Scripture tells us sinners will identify the "season" by recognizing the increasing birth pangs of a woman in labor. Analogous to the woman giving birth, the unholy final retribution for the damned will be Christ's return to punish them in Armageddon's battle. The Sinner's birth equivalent for delivering sin will be Hades and the Lake of Fire on the breathtaking day of the Lord when Jesus provides justice.

> Matthew 24 further states: [21] For then there will be great tribulation, such as has not been since the beginning of the world until this time, no, nor ever shall be." (1)

The above Scripture uses a future tense, "there _will be_ great tribulation, where the tense is future. Whereas below in Revelation, John witnesses the forthcoming event as it happens, i.e., _there was a great earthquake._ (Revelation 16:18)**_, such a mighty and great earthquake as had not occurred since men were on the earth._** Implied from Daniel 9/27, the Antichrist will agree to allow the Jews to rebuild their Temple just before the seven-year trial begins because it must exist to allow the sacrifice.

Two prophetic events will trigger the Tribulation:

> _(1)_ the **_Antichrist identifies himself_** by negotiating a 7-year peace with the "Many," Dan 9:27

> _(2)_ When the Antichrist takes over during the Great Tribulation years, meaning he had to have captured Israel and Jerusalem, he will immediately **_invoke the Abomination of desolation_** _by erecting a statue of himself to be the returned Christ and demanding Worship by churchgoers or death_

This sinful act will cause God to **have Jesus meet the saints in the air to Rapture them to their heavenly home** before unleashing God's wrath on those who have fallen away, the remnant sinners. Scripture argues that _all_ believers will go through some part of the tribulation.

(Matthew 24:30-31) We will see the Son of Man coming on the clouds of heaven with power and great glory to **_gather His elect from the four winds, from one end of heaven to the other._**

If the saved were raptured pre-trib, **_Satan would have no one left to persecute_**. However, the _left-behind_ will already take the Beast's mark as they willingly align with him.

Earlier in Matthew 24:22, it told us **_And unless those days were shortened, no flesh would be saved;_** but for the elect's sake, those days will be shortened.

These scriptures tell us we are all sinners, and to remain saved must confess our sins, repent and ask forgiveness through the blood of Jesus Christ. The Bible tells the "born again" their punishment will be a blessing via the Fifth Seal, in Revelation 6:9. These were the _[saved]_ souls of those under the altar, given white robes, martyred for their Godly belief. They cried out: "How long, O Lord, holy and true, until You judge and avenge our blood on those who dwell on the earth?" The response said they should rest a bit longer until the _death of their fellow servants and brethren_, that died as they _did, was completed [Comment: implied from the Great Tribulation_

God reserves the **_Great Tribulation's_** distinction for the _second three and a half years_ when He vents His wrath only on the remnant unbelievers to receive it. The previous Scripture defines the massive quake that occurred at Armageddon's time.

## Rebuilt Temple

While there have been many discussions about whether the Dome of the Rock houses Isaac's place of sacrifice on the same rock Muhammed took his ten-day journey to the heavens, one fact settles all the other arguments. The 1.5x1.5 square foot altar would be the highest point under the Dome, verified by measurement. Would God want the restored Temple built over the shrined Dome of the rock, knowing that the Antichrist would control it? I think not. I cannot believe our God would ever accept such a thing. Instead, I think he would build it next to the Dome of the Rock, based on a scripture that seems to pick its location by suggesting a temple with the gentiles' wall removed.

Since the Temple must exist for the Antichrist to permit Worship and sacrifice to the Jews, it must be available before the tribulation starts.

Furthermore, the False Prophet, when pursuing a single-world religion in harmony with the primary faiths: Christians, Jewish, and Muslims, Pope Francis <u>wrongly argues</u> that we are all children of the same GOD through the patriarch Abraham: we are not. Hypothetically, if we all worship the same GOD, religious wars will disappear, and the existing Pope is now doing his best to convince us this is true. However, parroting the best intent within all religions does not prove they come from the same Gods. The Pope is trying to persuade us that a religious consensus between the complying countries makes it factual: it does not. The agreement proclaims that the authors of such an idea get to determine what view is right or wrong. It denies that the only way to Heaven is through Jesus Christ by labeling it as religious or national extremism that cannot be tolerated by <u>"their group think"</u> consensus. In other words, they deny freedom of speech, only accepting what their group believes, disallowing anything else. It looks very much like our existing society.

### Man's and God's Calendar

I would argue that <u>*Revelation* 12</u> fulfillment on <u>*September 23, 2017,*</u> answers the **end of the age** questions asked by Jesus's disciples: "<u>*When will these things be?*</u>" and "<u>*what will be the sign of Your coming, and the end of the age?*</u>" Previously mentioned but not broadly appreciated, God's calendar is similar to ours. <u>*He has a comparable week for humanity that is 6000 years long*</u> (<u>*Peter 3:8–9*</u>). <u>*and has seeded many generations of humankind*</u> on our earth to test whether they would follow Him or Satan.

We are approaching the twilight of that 6-day week, literally the _end-of-days_ as it were: the time when Christ would soon return. Yet, with unusual worldwide goings-on, today's surroundings have troubled us with an unease we cannot explain, overlook, or even understand: something is wrong. If one knows the Bible, you know that our LORD God is warning us of the future retribution where His Son will arrive in the battle of Armageddon to judge, sort, and either reward or punish us. Several of His prophets tell us that as we enter these last days, we are not ready for His return and need to get our house in order.

**Genesis 6:3** in the Christian Bible confuses us when comparing it with the Jewish Torah.

> **Christian Bible (Genesis 6:3)** [3]And the Lord said, "My Spirit shall not strive[1] with man forever, for he _is_ indeed flesh; _yet his days shall be one hundred and twenty **years.**_" _[according to the Torah, it **should be Jubilee years,**_ i.e., 120x50 = 6000 years where one Jubilee year = 50 man-years].

From the Torah calendar website, it instead translates the same Scripture to mean:

> Torah **(Genesis 6:3)**: After 120 Jubilee Years, or 6000 years, He would no longer strive with mortal man. At the end of the sixth-millennium עשוהי, [6000 years], the Messiah will grant the gift of eternal Life - the age of Life to all who believe and obey Him.

The Bible translation suggests that the age limit of one hundred and twenty years is a human age. Simultaneously, the Torah indicates that the correct interpretation would have the LORD describe the period as Jubilee years. It would yield a 6000-year God's week consisting of "life ended by death," after which all who believe and obey God would inherit _eternal life_. Substituting the **2 Peter 3:8** definition of _"one day is as a thousand years"_ into man's week calendar validates the Torah interpretation by delivering a 6000-year week.

## God's Goal

What is God's goal? He wants as many souls in Heaven as possible and us to help Him get them there. He needs them to want unconditionally always to be with Him of their free will.

Thus, He will plant His seed throughout the church age to gauge how many will choose the LORD and become *"born again"* to be with Him. Others will find the Lake of Fire. Does not (Revelation 21:3-4) ultimately tell us what our LORD wants?

"Behold, the tabernacle of God is with men, and He will dwell with them, and they shall be His people. God, Himself will be with them and be their God. And God will wipe away every tear from their eyes; there shall be no more death, sorrow, or crying. There shall be no more pain, for the former things have passed away.

# WILL "BORN AGAIN" BELIEVERS EXPERIENCE THE TRIBULATION

While there may not be a direct Biblical statement that answers the question, many arguments suggest: Yes.

> (Romans 3:10} _argues_, "There is none righteous, no, **not one**,

(Matthew 24:22) scripture means that all flesh includes everyone: No one would survive otherwise. Since we are still here, all the days were shorter: ergo, if there was a threat, _we were all involved_ and, therefore, all experienced the tribulation.

This observation further implies that a pre-tribulation Rapture is not possible for two reasons:

Soon after the Abomination of Desolation by the Antichrist, those of us alive and dead in Christ, i.e., "born again," would be the elect taken up by god's angels to meet Jesus in the sky. In other words, it would be those who do God's work because they love him, not because they feel otherwise obligated.

> (James 2:18) But Someone will say, "You have faith, and I have works." Show me your faith without your works, and I will show you my faith by my works.

Nonbelievers would be left behind under Satan.

**Lest we forget,**

this discussion is totally in the future.

(**Daniel 10:14**) [14] Now, I have come to make you understand what will happen to your people in the latter days, for the vision refers to many days yet to come.

(**Daniel 8:17**): [17] So he came near where I stood, and when he came I was afraid and fell on my face, but he said to me, "Understand, son of man, that the vision refers to the time of the end." (1)

(**Matt 24:15**) and (**Luke 21:20**): When we see standing in the Holy Place the **Abomination of desolation** (Antichrist Image), spoken of by Daniel, and see Jerusalem surrounded with armies, then flee to the mountains.

## DANIEL'S PROPHECY

Daniel's forecast is one of the most important scriptures in the Bible. Between the years of 521 to 486 BC, Daniel, while praying for Jerusalem,

"[19] O Lord, hear! O Lord, forgive!"

Daniel received a vision from the angel Gabriel that he should prophesy a 490-year punishment for his people and the holy city. It further predicted the death of Christ, and when Pilate crucified Him after only 483 years, that act deferred the completion of the last 7-year week of Daniel's Timeline sentence until Israel once again became a nation. Timewise, the Messiah would be "cut off:" (crucified), 483 prophetic years after the Decree given by King Artaxerxes on March 5, 444BC (Gregorian calendar). Thus, the last 70th (7-year) week would be known as "The Tribulation." It now becomes apparent why God saved the 70th week for the future.

### Daniel's Timeline

Four or five years ago, I prayed to God to clarify ***Daniel's rapture/tribulation timeline***. He instantly gave me the answer. I knew then that there could be no pre-trib or post-trib solution, but I had not discovered the scriptural connection until several years ago. There are enough intricate relationships that will not divulge their secrets willingly with only a casual read: it takes some study. My problem is that I have become too close to the topic over the nine years and had not used adequate explanations because I felt the readers knew more than they did. In this document, I have tried to correct that error.

The image clarifies the numbering theme for the 7-year tribulation. Sequential periods in days, months, years, or 3.5-year increments define the time. The plotting of the four scriptures below the graph **_shows_** that the Rapture and other interpretations are Biblical. Daniel's 9:27 Timeline noted that two consecutive 3.5-year periods comprise the seven years. The _first 3.5 years_ is the _Wrath of the Lamb,_ where Jesus opens the (Revelation 6) Seals describing those judgments. _The second 3.5-year period_ is the _Wrath of God,_ where His angels deliver the Trumpet (Revelation 8) and Bowl (Revelation 16), punishments similar to the Plagues of Exodus

The above image clarifies the 7-year tribulation represented in days, months, years, or 3.5-year increments.

The scriptural lines

- In prophecy, a prophetic _month_ is 30 days.
- The time for a prophetic _year_ then becomes 12x30 =360 days
- time times and one-half time = "time = 1 year, + times =2 years + ½ time = 1/2 year _= 3.5 years_
- 42 months = 42/12 months/year _= 3.5 years_
- 1260 days = 1260/ 360 days/year _= 3.5 years_

Timeline Graph Scripture

> **(Dan 9:27)** But in the middle of the week He shall bring an end to sacrifice and offering.."
>
> **(Dan 7:25)** For a time and times and half a time.
>
> **(Dan 12:11-12)** one thousand three hundred and thirty-five days.
>
> **(Rev 11:1-3)** one thousand two hundred and sixty days, clothed in sackcloth."

**Dan 8:13-14** "For two thousand three hundred [b]days; then the sanctuary shall be cleansed

## Daniel's Timeline Image

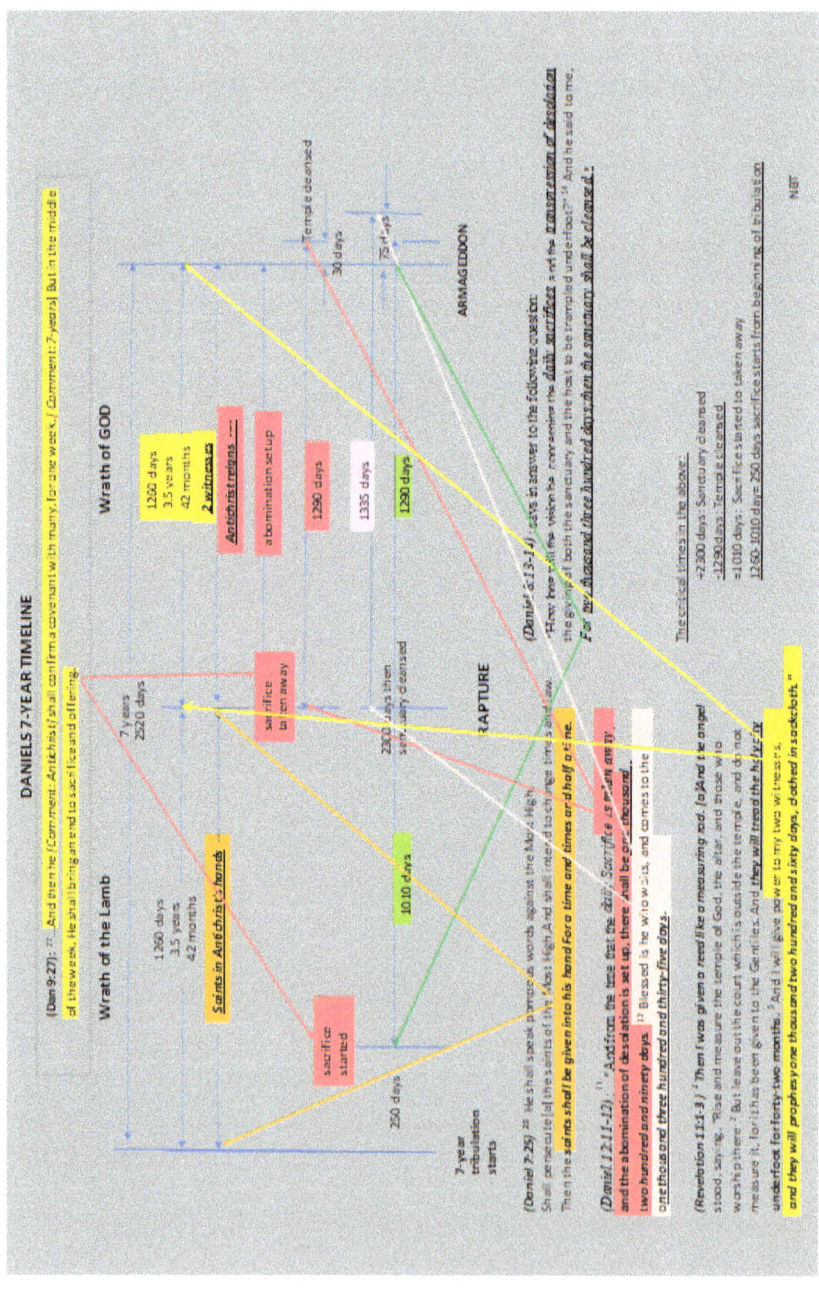

Daniel 9:25-27

[25] "Know therefore and understand, *That* from the going forth of the command To restore and build Jerusalem Until Messiah the Prince,

**There shall be seven weeks and sixty-two weeks;**
**[Comment: 69x7=483 years from the start of building the walls to His crucifixion]**

> The [h]street shall be built again, and the [i]wall, Even in troublesome times. [26] "And after the sixty-two weeks [Comment: 483 years] Messiah shall [j]be cut off, but not for Himself; And the <u>people</u> [Muslims] of the prince [Antichrist] who is to come Shall destroy the city and the sanctuary. The end of it *shall be* with a flood, And till the end of the war, desolations are determined.

### The 490-year Decree

In the Decree that straddles the transition from the *age of law* to the *church's age*, God, through His Grace, grants His disciples time to end their transgressions and get themselves "right" with Him by resolving the six issues in Daniel's prophecy. Historically, the Jewish people had not obeyed the LORD resulting in their punishment of scattering them to the ends of the Earth, as quoted in:

> Deuteronomy 28:64. Only in Israel's May 1947 rebirth did they again become a nation prophesied by (Isaiah 66:8) [8]"Who has heard such a thing? Who has seen such things? Shall the earth be made to give birth in one day? Or shall a nation be born at once?"

**With the stroke of a pen, the last week, "the tribulation," could begin again**. The prophesied punishment commences with the "falling away" from the Church and the Antichrist revealing himself.

It starts with a subtle comment from Satan; we should expect it to be a lie. But, first, he promised a 7-year covenant treaty with the many and then defaulted on his promise halfway through the seven years.

*Note that it would set the 3.5-year mark.*

Second, implicitly it tells us that the Antichrist would allow the Jews their sacrifices and offerings during the 1st 3.5 years: implying a rebuilt temple on the Temple Mount. Bringing an end to the Jews' sacrifice would have to happen because the Antichrist captured Israel/Jerusalem.

## Daniel: a *future* event

The statement of Daniel 9:27 is a "Calm before the Storm" Scripture. With a casual read, it would even seem easy to dismiss it. However, by God's standards, it is one of the essential pieces of Scripture in the Bible. If we do not understand what it means, we won't know what to expect in the end-times.

> (Daniel 8:17): [17]So he came near where I stood, and when he came I was afraid and fell on my face, but he said to me, "*Understand, son of man,* **that the vision refers to the time of the end.**"

Palestine and some of its close allies would never relent from eradicating Israel. This fact lies boldly in front of us as Daniel 9:27 tells its story, pointing to the coming spiritual war between God and Satan. Historically, the beast nations have always been the same since God gave Abraham the promised land: Syria, Iraq, Iran, Turkey, Greece, Egypt, Libya, Ethiopia/ Cush, Sudan, and Lebanon. Most of these nations will be the ones who promise to dedicate themselves to the future cause of re-establishing the past Ottoman caliphate.

## The 70TH Week End-Time Prophecy

When would the ***tribulation*** start: -- i.e., the 70th week, the last seven years? First, everyone wants to know where we are now and what happens as we progress through Revelation's many symbolic events.

Because of Israel's transgressions, God defined a 490-year punishment that Israel must suffer because of its sinfulness and lack of repentance. Their journey through that testing time begins with Daniel's extraordinary vision and prophecies.

It describes 70x7 weeks (490 years), a sentence that truncates one week early at the end of 483 years: the nagging question – why? The 490 years was a probationary period where our Father expected Israel to make itself "right" with Him. Once the end-time clock starts again, the prophecy states it will be a time of great distress, which man has never seen before. The remaining week of punishment will begin after the Jewish people's prophesied regathering in Israel's rebirth. Why the massive gap in time? -- Interpretation of Daniel 9 explains it.

## Wrath of the Lamb

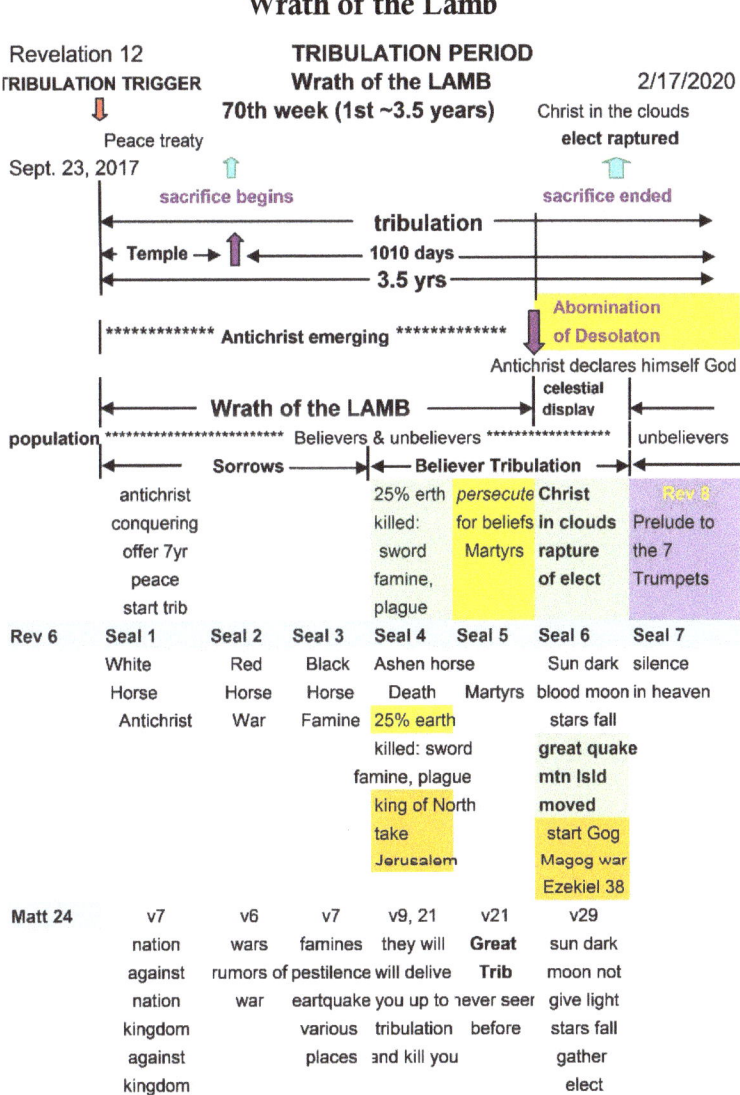

| Revelation 12 TRIBULATION TRIGGER | **TRIBULATION PERIOD** **Wrath of the LAMB** **70th week (1st ~3.5 years)** | 2/17/2020 Christ in the clouds elect raptured |

Peace treaty — Sept. 23, 2017

sacrifice begins — sacrifice ended

tribulation

Temple — 1010 days — 3.5 yrs

************ Antichrist emerging *************

**Abomination of Desolaton**

Antichrist declares himself God

celestial display

—— Wrath of the LAMB ——

population ************************ Believers & unbelievers ***************** | unbelievers

—— Sorrows —→ ←— Believer Tribulation —→

| | | | | | | | |
|---|---|---|---|---|---|---|---|
| antichrist conquering offer 7yr peace start trib | | | 25% erth killed: sword famine, plague | *persecute* for beliefs Martyrs | Christ in clouds rapture of elect | Rev 8 Prelude to the 7 Trumpets | |
| **Rev 6** | **Seal 1** White Horse Antichrist | **Seal 2** Red Horse War | **Seal 3** Black Horse Famine | **Seal 4** Ashen horse Death 25% earth killed: sword famine, plague king of North take Jerusalem | **Seal 5** Martyrs | **Seal 6** Sun dark blood moon stars fall great quake mtn Isld moved start Gog Magog war Ezekiel 38 | **Seal 7** silence in heaven |
| **Matt 24** | v7 nation against nation kingdom against kingdom | v6 wars rumors of war | v7 famines pestilence eartquake various places | v9, 21 they will will delive you up to tribulation and kill you | v21 **Great** **Trib** never seer before | v29 sun dark moon not give light stars fall gather elect | |

# WRATH OF THE LAMB (1st 3.5 years)

In judging us for the first 3.5-years, Jesus will break the seals on the scroll to unleash pain and suffering on the unrighteous, likened to the travail of a pregnant woman in her early months. I believe the Antichrist has already identified himself during the fulfillment of Revelation 12 on September 23, 2017, which is the tribulation start date. We are approaching the third year in the first 3.5-year period. Rebuilding the Temple is one of the prerequisites that has not yet started. But it must be standing for the Antichrist to perform his Abomination of desolation.

The Antichrist will have to be very proud of himself in this beginning period. He promises to unite the Muslim nations and Israel in harmony for the first time when he finishes the Peace treaty with the "many." Naturally, participants would herald the moment as a world-shaking event, but the initial effort would fall short because of not overcoming the Islamic nation's hate. The following should further show doubters the validity of the preceding claim that the Antichrist will control God's "followers" for only 3.5 years.

## 1st PROOF

Summary: The need to shorten the elect's punishment days so all would not die is satisfied by Rapturing immediately after the 1st 3.5 years, thereby shortening their years by avoiding the last 3.5 years on earth. The Saints will be in the Antichrist's hand for only those first 3.5 years.

## 2nd PROOF

God shows the parallelism between Matthew 24:29 and Revelation 6:12, covering the same celestial event of the sun turning black and the moon red, indicating that the Rapture will happen at Mid-tribulation.

Parallel Scriptures of the same celestial event

> (Matthew 24) starts with "Immediately after the tribulation of those days." [i.e., after Seals 1-6 of Revelation 6]

(Matthew 24); the sun will be darkened, and the moon will not give its light; the stars will fall from heaven, [the stars are angels who collect the raptured] and the powers of the heavens will be shaken.

(Revelation 1-6) and the sun became black as sackcloth of hair, and the [h]moon became like blood, 13 And the stars of heaven fell to the earth, [the stars are angels who collect the raptured as a fig tree drops its late figs when it is shaken by a mighty wind. 14 Then the sky [i]**receded** as a scroll [rapture happening] when it is rolled up, and every mountain and island was moved out of its place. [Rapture dream experience of Pastor Carl Gallups of Hickory Hammock Baptist Church in Milton, Florida.]

(Matthew 24); Son of Man in the Clouds: "Rapture" they will see the **Son of Man** coming on the clouds of heaven with power and great glory. 31 And He will send His angels with a great sound of a trumpet, and they will gather together [Rapture] His [d]elect from the four winds, from one end of heaven to the other.

Summary: Matthew 24 and Revelation 6 describe the same celestial event as "immediately after the tribulation of those days." It occurs when the massive Nibiru system will be between our sun and us, crossing our planetary system ecliptic, i.e., the plane of all our planets rotating around the sun: thus, blackening the earth and moon's view. This enormous system will also cause an earthquake that moves the mountains and the islands out of their place.

Then God will send Christ to appear to us to bring all of His elect to heaven, i.e., RAPTURE them.

Matthew 24 30 Then the sign of the Son of Man will appear in heaven, and then all the tribes of the earth will mourn, and they will see the Son of Man coming on the clouds of heaven with power and great glory. 31 And He will send His angels with a great sound of a trumpet, and they will gather together His [d]elect from the four winds, from one end of heaven to the other.

Key Phrase: "Immediately after the tribulation of those days." [i.e., after Seals 1-6 of Revelation 6] Christ will appear in the clouds and RAPTURE the elect.

## 3rd PROOF

Reaching back to a much earlier time, Matthew 24:15-21: references Daniel 11's wars between the King of the north, Syria, and King of the South, Egypt, in 167BCE. The Abomination of desolation occurs when the Syrian King sacrifices a pig to Zeus in God's sanctuary. However, the Phrase only appears once in Matthew, Mark, and Daniel, where it becomes the model from 167BC for what will happen when our 2022+ Antichrist counterpart shows his face.

The Great Tribulation, the final period, displays the Abomination of Desolation in the Holy Temple for the last 3.5 years leading to Armageddon.

> Matthew 24 [15] "Therefore when you see the 'abomination of desolation,' spoken of by Daniel the prophet, standing in the holy place" (whoever reads, let him understand), [16] "then let those who are in Judea flee to the mountains [21] For then there will be great tribulation, such as has not been since the beginning of the world until this time, no, nor ever shall be.

Key Phrase:: Daniel 9:27, But in the middle of the week, He shall bring an end to sacrifice and offering. And place there the abomination of desolation. It is the Scripture that defines Daniel's Tribulation/Rapture Timeline proving that if the Antichrist owns the last 3.5 years, then the Saints could only be in his hands for the first 3.5 years

### Antichrist captures Israel/Jerusalem

Satan's plot for the end-time capture of Israel/Jerusalem started in approximately 167BCE and has yet to occur in our time. However, the exploits of Antiochus 1V in Daniel 11 establish the model that Scripture will follow. Our 2022+ Antichrist's capturing of Israel/Jerusalem would occur around the 4th Seal of Revelation 6, which indicates a 25% loss of Life for all reasons. The Seals describe the coming of a conqueror on a white horse in the 1st Seal followed by a fiery red horse in the 2nd Seal destroying peace, trailed by a 3rd Seal, a black horse, predicting famine, as a natural byproduct of the first three. Such account results in the persecution of the souls involved, appearing in Seal 5 as the martyrs under the heavenly altar calling out to God for vengeance.

Satan plans to emulate in 2022+ what Antiochus did in overcoming Israel/ Jerusalem in 167BCE. We are now in the first stages of our tribulation, with the Antichrist starting to emerge as described in Seal 1. 2nd

Seal destroying peace trailed by a 3rd Seal,

While the expected peace treaty with the "many" called out in Daniel 9:27 has not yet occurred, it has to be on a shortlist of things to happen. As told in Daniel, Satan never intends to honor his promise of peace between the Jews and their Muslim neighbors. Instead, he plans to emulate Antiochus' behavior through our 2022+ yet-to-appear Antichrist.

Antiochus erected an altar dedicated to the Greek god Zeus with his accompanying image to worship. Our Antichrist will do the same: place a replication of himself in the sanctuary to worship under the threat of death.

Antiochus IV, in Daniel 11, was the notorious King of the North who performed the previous Jewish Temple desecration in 167 BC. His clashes with Ptolemy of Egypt occurred roughly in 330 -164 BCE. Over time, he emerged from Syria to become one of the military leaders under Alexander the Great of Greece. When Alexander died, Antiochus received Babylonia and Alexander's eastern provinces to form the Seleucid Empire, including central Anatolia, Persia, the Levant, and Mesopotamia. Thus, it appears he was the first from those early empires, with a string of Syrian and Ptolemaian dynasties continuously using Israel as a passageway for their battles. Daniel 11 describes those battles between the King of the North, Syria, and Egypt's South.

While Daniel 11 accurately portrayed the battles and intrigue from verses 1 through 39, we will see those verses 40 through 50 cause us to leap into the future using "today's" King of the North and the South definitions. Also, note that we are indeed at the end of time:

> Daniel 12:9 He replied, "Go your way, Daniel because the words are rolled up and sealed until the time of the end.

> (Daniel 11:40-45) [40] "At the time of the end, [Comment: that Phrase only used once in the Bible, refers to the end of God's 6000 year week,] the King of the South [Today's Egypt and allies] shall attack him; and the new King of the North [neo-Ottoman Caliphat] shall come against him like a whirlwind, with chariots, horsemen, and with many ships; and he shall enter the countries, overwhelm them, and pass through. [41] He shall also enter the Glorious Land, and many countries shall be overthrown; but these shall escape from his hand: Edom, Moab, and the prominent people of Ammon. [42] He shall stretch out his hand against the countries, and the land of Egypt shall not escape. [43] He shall have power over the treasures of gold and silver, and over all the precious things of Egypt; also the Libyans and Ethiopians shall follow at his heels. [44]But news from the east and the north shall trouble him; therefore, he shall go out with great fury to destroy and annihilate many. [45]And he shall plant the tents of his Palace between the seas and the glorious holy mountain; yet he shall come to his end, and no one will help him.

The Antichrist has changed from the 167BCE Antiochus to a first version of the 2022+ neo-Ottoman entity where verse 45 says "he came to his end," which implies his death. God incarnate and His army begin attacking Gog-Magog when He returned with "all His Saints" in Zech 14:5. Ezekiel 38-39 covers God's grudge against Satanic forces by referring to Himself as the LORD GOD, saying: "I *am* against you, O Gog." Also, He asks a rhetorical question:

> Ezekiel 38:16-17 [16] It will be in the latter days that I will bring you against My land, so that the nations may know

GOD - The Here And The HEREAFTER

Me, when I am hallowed in you, O Gog, before their eyes." [17] Thus says the Lord God: "Are you, [Gog] he of whom I have spoken in <u>former days</u> by My servants the prophet of Israel, who prophesied for years in those days that I would bring you against them

Furthermore, the prophetic time was when "a people gathered from the nations," which collected the Jews to Israel, making it a nation again in 1947. It would set the stage for:

Matthew 24:34, "this generation will by no means pass away till all these things take place."

The Scripture alludes to all the judgments that must happen in Revelations prophesies to finish the end of God's 6000-year week. Daniel 11:45 sets the time of spiritual transformation where our 2022+ Antichrist, who represents the neo-Ottoman Caliphate instead of Antiochus, appears in the tents of the Palace between the Mediterranean and the Dead Sea, having just overcome Israel and take the Holy City. But God answers in retribution, and the verse <u>"He shall come to his end, and no one will help him"</u> scripturally tells us that He does away with the Antichrist and buries him in Hamon-Gog.

The LORD GOD has destroyed the Antichrist armies west of the Euphrates, but not the yet prophesied armies of Armageddon.

Would there be a peace treaty after defeating the Gog-Magog beast country and its allies? After all, a nuclear war decimated the countryside and contaminated considerable territory, and Armageddon has not even happened yet.

There is no indication in the Bible, but a dialog between Clare Dubois and Jesus suggests through online prophetic ministries that there would be a treaty after the Rapture that was not the treaty offered by the Antichrist

Since God incarnate defeated the western Antichrist army, <u>only the Armageddon forces east of the Euphrates would be the threat left for God's army to face.</u>

> (Joel 2) tells us: "*But I* [God] *will remove far from you* **[Jewish people]** the northern army, **[Turkey Iran, etc. new King of the north --- neo-Ottoman ten nations.]** *And will drive him away into a barren and desolate land, With his face toward the eastern sea* **[Sea of Galilee]** *And his back toward the western sea* **[Mediterannian]**; *His stench* **[God's supernatural attack on neo-Ottoman Caliphate, etc. Armageddon]** *will come up, And his foul odor will rise Because he has done* [h]*monstrous things.*"

God had trapped the Antichrist's army in Megiddo between the Mediterranean and the Sea of Galilee. That army had grown from the early Syrian Beast to a neo-Ottoman Empire Caliphate that picked up ten Muslim nations in acquiring its size. It became the new King of the North, formerly the beastly name for Antiochus, in 168 BC. Thus, it became known as Gog-Magog or the neo-Ottoman Caliphate.

Had we believed the war between the King of the north and Egypt took place in 168 BCE, Antiochus would have died in Judea battling the Jews. Instead, history tells us Antiochus perished in a campaign against the emerging Parthian Empire in Persia, killing him in 164 BC. The end-time event is yet to come and is placed in the oncoming years of 2022+, and verses 40-45 reflect the future since Antiochus did not die in Judea. Would it be Daniel's beyond? This monster will be the new grown-up Beast described earlier, born out of the Ottoman Empire and killed by being on the wrong side in WW1. It would be grown from 10 uncommitted countries' promises to support the neo-Ottoman Caliphate in the upcoming battle with Christ at Armageddon. Because Gog-Magog plays an early part in Satan's plan to capture Israel/Jerusalem, it is pertinent to describe his intentions and how they relate to the latter role during the final 3.5 years.

## Judgments [Wheat or Tares]

While we touched on God's goal of getting us to heaven, we would like to know how this process of separating the Wheat and the Tares fits Daniel's Timeline. After all, we are talking about the second chance, i.e., Rapture, to bring more souls to heaven. Before Christ, Abraham believed in God, and that belief, faith, counted for him as righteous" and was his path to heaven as it would be for any other believer. Given that GOD is all about harvesting souls in getting them to Heaven, it would seem reasonable to define some spiritual terms. We are a combination of flesh and Spirit, where the soul and the Holy Spirit simultaneously occupy the same space when fitting into one's glove-like body. The Spirit and soul transfer to Heaven, while one's remains to stay on Earth. These spirits in us proclaim we are a Temple of God, consistent with the Bible.

God has close to 2000 years from the crucifixion until now to resolve who will make the Rapture. Moreover, He has a life span of 70-80 years from Scripture to make the judgment.

> Psalm 90:10 [10] The days of our lives are seventy years; And if by reason of strength they are eighty years, Yet their boast is only labor and sorrow; For it is soon cut off, and we fly away.

His first "sort" will occur during the Rapture, where God's good and bad seeds are analogous to the Wheat and tares' harvest at the end of the age. God tells the reapers: "First gather the tares and bind them together in bundles to burn, but gather the wheat into my barn."

"The Wrath of the Lamb" will deliver God's first end-time harvest by separating "good" (Wheat) and "evil" (tares) and Rapture those who are "Born Again." Generations of winnowing would separate the Wheat from the tares to select all His souls. Then, like Jesus's resurrection, the Raptured "born again" would inherit their glorified body upon arriving in Heaven.

## 1ST JUDGING: humanity

Who? Population:

Adam/Eve                 to Rapture

Good/Bad Metaphor:       Wheat vs. tares

Period covered:          3.5years short of 6000

Salvation criteria:      "born again."

War:                     numerous over 6000 years

# FALSE WORSHIP STARTED

For Christians, the handwriting is already on the wall. Throughout the Pope's papacy, he has laid the groundwork for a one-world religion: -- but scarcely anyone seems to care. The Bible, prophesying such happenings for the end-times, admits the majority will embrace the Antichrist. Since evidence is already starting to accumulate, it reaffirms we are looking at the end of god's week. The Pope supports Chrislam, a combination of Christianity and Islam. Already 72 churches in the U.S. practice that false religion. Reasonably, the Pope could show that Christians and other religions could independently worship, in the shared rebuilt Temple, each honoring their god according to their traditions. However, when the Antichrist consolidates his power and invokes the Beast's mark, he will declare himself the returned Christ via the Abomination of desolation when he presents his image for followers to worship under the threat of death. Notwithstanding, Israel wants the Temple because it was also part of their eschatological Covenant with God. On the other hand, Muslims need the Antichrist (their Mahdi) to perform his Abomination of desolation, declaring himself God in the Jewish sanctuary.

How the third Temple gets rebuilt will be God's decision, not the Jews or the Muslims.

Mysteriously the Bible itself seems to offer the northern possibility arguing that the site will be under the enemy's control for the last 3.5 years, so there is no need for the court of the Gentiles. Without the wall, it would fit nicely just north of the Dome. Also, I would guess that God would not want His Holy ground ever under the evil one's control.

## Gog-Magog location

Gog-Magog is nothing more than a different name for the grown-up Beast. Who are they, and from where did they come? Bible atlases, IVP Atlas of Bible History, New Moody Atlas of the Bible, The Holman Bible

Atlas, Zondervan, Atlas of the Bible, and others list <u>Magog in Turkey</u>. The phrase "Gog of the land of Magog" refers to Gog as a leader of Magog's land that includes Turkey and its allies: i.e., the Neo-Ottoman Caliphate. Daniel 8 and 11 are parallel scriptures to Ezekiel 38-39. They both describe future attacks on Israel, i.e., "In the latter years." (Ezekiel 38:8). At the time of the end (Daniel 11:40). The <u>new </u>King of the North shall come against the South (Egypt) like a whirlwind and enter the Glorious Land (Israel). <u>Egypt, Libya,</u> and <u>Ethiopia</u> <u>will be</u> [future tense] captured. The New King of the North shall plant the tents of his Palace between the seas and the glorious holy mountain, <u>yet he shall come to his end, and no one will help him</u> (Dan 11:45). The implication is that Israel is under siege or taken by the <u>new</u> undefined <u>King of the North,</u> with <u>Egypt, Libya,</u> and <u>Ethiopia </u>as captured allies.

Note that <u>Libya and Ethiopia are both the New King of the North and the Gog-Magog identity in Ezekiel 38:5, meaning they are the same.</u> Two different entities cannot own identical armies: Therefore, Gog-Magog is the new King of the North – the Beast from the sea – the new <u>neo-Ottoman</u> Beast that will follow the will of the Antichrist in attacking Israel in the end-days. As noted earlier, the <u>offending countries</u> have not changed over time, only the names.

> (Ezekiel 38:7-9) [5]Persia, <u>Ethiopia, and Libya are</u> with them, all of them with shield and helmet; [6] Gomer and all its troops; <u>the house of Togarmah from the far north</u> and all its troops-many people are with you. [7] "Prepare yourself and be ready, you and all your companies that are gathered about you; and be a guard for them. [8] After many days you will be visited. In the latter years you will come into the land of those brought back from the sword and gathered from many people on the mountains of Israel, which had long been desolate; they were brought out of the nations, and now all of them dwell safely.[9] You will ascend, coming like a storm, covering the land like a cloud, you and all your troops and many peoples with you."

So the scriptural alignment of Islamic countries starting to form the neo-Ottoman Beast are Turkey, Persia (Iran), Egypt, Libya, and Ethiopia;

virtually surrounding Israel as warned by Luke 21 with Gog as the Antichrist heading the Gog-Magog attack on Israel/Jerusalem

(Luke 21:20,24): The Destruction of Jerusalem

This regional conflict will be the modern-day battle for Israel and the Holy City. And then, It will morph into the Gog-Magog war covering the last 3.5 years. It must start just before mid-tribulation to allow Satan's victory that permits setting up the Abomination of Desolation in the rebuilt Temple. In so doing, it will initiate the latter half, the Great Tribulation of God's Wrath. Then, as we shall see, it will again morph into Armageddon: ending in THE DAY OF THE LORD, where His anger stops just short of destroying the earth. The coming Antichrist will emulate Antiochus IV Epiphanes' prior 168 BC desecration in our children's lifetime.

## ABOMINATION OF DESOLATION IMAGE

Verses 36-39 of Daniel 11 describe Antiochus's pillaging and devastation of Israel/Jerusalem. Verse 40 explicitly says: "At the time of the end," leaving no doubt that verses 40-45 will cover the Antichrist's spirit's transition into the future. Having a natural hatred of the Jews following their covenant with God, he outlawed the faithful's religious rites and traditions by ordering them to worship Zeus as the supreme god (2 Maccabees 6:1–12). This desecrating act of sacrificing a pig on the altar in the Holy Place of the Jewish Temple resulted in the Biblical term "Abomination of desolation," where people were told they must worship the idol of Zeus or die. Because the Jews refused to obey, Antiochus severely persecuted them by sending an army to enforce his Decree. They slaughtered many and destroyed Jerusalem because of their resistance. Antiochus's persecution of the Jews in Jerusalem was between 168 to 167 BC. The following verses, 40-45, imply one thing, but the reality is something else. Scholars claim that the above verses are historically correct, but, as previously suggested, there is a mystery in the last five scriptures 40-45: They are future, not 167BC.

## The Mark of the Beast

Seal 4 shows the ravages of the first three seals, where famine results in food scarcity, causing widespread hunger and producing death through starvation. Ensuing battles would further worsen the growing body count. The image left would be the beasts of the Earth graphically feasting on the slaughter left by the Apocolypse's White, Red, Black, and Pale Horses. The Antichrist would expand these deaths across nations by employing the Beast's mark. The population could not buy or sell without taking the "mark." Satan's followers would behead believing families who would rather accept that fate than deny their Lord.

The Lord told His prophet, Sadhu, that He would like to see him start Martyrism schools to teach the children about the glory of martyrdom rather than living in fear of their sacrifice. Beheading believers may sound gruesome, but they arrive in Heaven never feeling the blade. The Spirit is out of the body before the pain hits. If you train your children to expect the immediate blessings of Heaven in Martyrism, Satan cannot use your child's fear against you to forsake your faith and take the mark. Instead of suffering the fear of death, the children now know, and parents should tell their children to say to the terrorists: Jesus loves you before their heinous act. The "mark" caused the martyred souls from under the altar in Seal 5 to cry to God to avenge their deaths for keeping their faith. They would receive white robes acknowledging their sacrifice while learning that they would have to wait for God's vengeance a while until their future martyred brethren would join them. Most of the dead would likely be the Christians and Jews lost in the battle for Israel. However, the 25% deaths would also include those from the upcoming Gog-Magog war that would continue to increase the slaughter as Yahweh fights his former allies. All these deaths would happen after the three days of darkness that will occur just before the Rapture

### Three days of darkness/demons

For what purpose is the Plague of Darkness? During Exodus, the Lord hardened the Pharoah's heart for not humbling himself before the Lord nor releasing His people from slavery to serve Him. So He had Moses punish them by putting the plague of darkness on the land for not letting his people go.

Exodus 10 The Plague of Darkness

[21]Then the Lord said to Moses, "Stretch out your hand toward the sky so that darkness spreads over Egypt—darkness that can be felt." [22]So Moses stretched out his hand toward the sky, and total darkness covered all of Egypt for three days. [23]No one could see anyone else or move about for three days. Yet all the Israelites had light in the places where they lived.

Appearing to be parallel Scripture to Revelation 6:6 are the following.

(Joel 2:2) Blow the [a]trumpet in Zion, And sound an alarm in My holy mountain! Let all the inhabitants of the land tremble; For the day of the Lord is coming, For it is at hand: [2]A day of darkness and gloominess, A day of clouds and thick darkness, Like the morning clouds spread over the mountains. Yet, a people come, great and strong, The like of whom has never been; Nor will there ever be any such after them, Even for many successive generations.

(Amos 5:18) [18]Woe to you who long for the day of the Lord! Why do you long for the day of the Lord? It will be darkness, not light.

Similarly, our Lord meant to do the same thing in the following circumstance. Many prophetic blogs occur on the internet where God has contacted dedicated Christians by giving them visions or dreams of things to come. They may have received them in the past, but He will request they share them with others sometime in the future. I started writing this book from such a vision and have no problem believing the miraculous stories that have yet to happen: I am still living mine. Immediately to follow is another.

Linda Courtney's Story

The sun turns black with the moon red, and the days of darkness start – the first pass of the Nibiru system. In the three days of the night preceding the Rapture, God's army of demons begins to attack the unrighteous while the righteous remain in their homes under lock and key with shaded windows for those days. It will be the last time the wicked have a chance to repent and cry to God to include them in the Rapture.

One early morning, Linda Courtney was praying to our Lord Jesus when suddenly, He told her to write. Again, she was reluctant, but He repeated the request, and finally, she complied. As a result, she wrote five pages on "the three days and nights of darkness." Following is her story. God's warning to those who will listen to prepare for this traumatic event will occur before the Rapture.

## God's Message

God says I am The Good Shepherd. This area of time, as humanity knows time, is coming to its end. As of a few days from now, everything is coming to its sudden change. The time of profound transition is soon to come upon the entire Earth. The scientists will call it Earth or climate change. But, I, the Lord God Almighty, call it my holy will and the fulfillment of my holy and most profound decrees, which have been established from time immemorial. I am the great I am. The feeble mortal hand of man can do nothing to alter, hinder, or stop what I have prepared for humanity. My plan shall stand. Indeed, this error of humanity's journey on Earth is quickly coming to a close as I change and rearrange all things.

This Earth will soon enter a time of severe global darkness. People will understand as I, the Almighty God, draw the curtain of black upon the planet. Those people of mine who have heard of this word will understand. I will grab the sudden attention of humanity as all the technology comes to a sudden incapacitating ability to function. All will be silent, and humanity will be thrown into sudden disarray. They will panic as confusion occurs. Many people will lose rational thinking as the curtain of gross darkness covers the Earth.

I, the Lord God, must do this literally to grab the attention of all the citizens of Earth. My people, those who know Jesus Christ as their Lord and Savior, will be shaken far less than the Sinner. They will be stabilized by my Holy Spirit as the unction of my holy presence falls upon them. My Holy Spirit will calm their minds as they falter for a while, gathering their wits about them. So, see, my beloved children, there are millions of Christians who are saved by my grace that have never heard of the Days of Darkness. That's why I'm calling upon you to tell them what is just around the bend. You may approach it with scientific terms, for I will indeed use natural means to create this phenomenon. My planet, which many call Planet X or Nibiru, is stealing its way to cover your sun eventually. This planet has been observed in various places on Earth at times with the naked eye. When this planet covers your sun when this occurs, I will, in my great mercy, hold and totally control the Earth's temperature at 55 degrees so that no man or animal will freeze.

(Linda Courtney interjecting: because if a planet would cover the sun, normally speaking, we would be thrown into an ice age, but God Himself is going to control the temperature in His mercy upon the Earth.

The Holy Spirit says, however, cold will be felt. So, gather blankets for warmth, food, and water for medical needs if necessary. They must be out there ready. Do not discount this warning, for you will need food and water unless you choose to fast. Candles must be white and unscented. Do not question me over this. Oil lights may be used. Use refined oil as much as possible. Listen well, my beloved ones, I am your Holy Father in Heaven; You have no earthly Holy Father. The Pope of Rome is not holy, for I alone am holy. These days of gross darkness are my great act of mercy to get the full attention of Mankind. At that time, many of the world's false gods will fall.

Those who worship any false God will have the blinders removed, and they will be able to choose me as Lord God and Savior if they so desire. However, the ultimate choice will still be theirs as I force no one to surrender to me.

Listen further, my beloved ones. Immediately before this darkness falls, the Earth will quake. The Earth will quake as it groans for the manifestation of the sons of God. In many places, there will be actual earthquakes occurring. As the darkness descends, there will be majestic displays in the cosmos. I, the Lord God Almighty, the Lord Jesus Christ God in the flesh, will rearrange the skies for humanity to see the glorious colors and the deep blood-red as the colors wander around the Earth. They will see this phenomenon that has never been seen before. I have reserved it for this time.

Planet X will bring great earth changes as the atmosphere will be charged with electricity. This will not hurt or kill humankind, but they can see this as a discharge that will be intense. When these changes begin to occur in the heavens, you are to notify your loved ones immediately. They are to drop whatever they're doing and immediately come to their home. It is (now Listen importantly) best if family members can be together in the house of one of the believers in Yeshua Jesus Christ.

This is why I desire that you tell them beforehand what's coming to the Earth, so they are willing to cooperate with you when the time arrives. Otherwise, they will call you crazy and not come into your home.

(Linda Courtney: interjecting. In other words, when we see the aurora borealis or the bright red stripes in the sky and the lightning out of season with all these cosmic displays. Then we should call our loved ones and say, hey, this is the time. Come before it turns dark in a day or two or whatever. You better get into my home with me. They're going to say: are you kidding, this is just an earth change. The scientists say the Earth is going to go through changes, so you're crazy. This reason is why we're supposed to tell our people beforehand. Getting on with the word from the Lord)

I desire you to alert them now for their sake. During these three days and nights of darkness, many unsaved people will indeed receive, Yeshua, Jesus Christ, as their Savior if they have laid a good foundation. Now is the time for us to be evangelists: not to wait until the darkness falls because then it will be too late. We won't be able to go out of our homes. So now is our time to get on with the word of the Spirit of <u>God</u>.

As you enter your home, <u>I admonish you to cover your windows and do not look out at all periods.</u> Do not look out at all. <u>Lock your doors,</u> and <u>do not open them to anyone.</u> Why? You ask my beloved children. I will tell you why. <u>During this time, I will allow hordes of demons to roam the entire Earth. People from all nationalities will be aware of this, and many will die from fear and demonic torment or attack. Also, the seas will roar, and great will be the changes that torment sinful humanity. For my beloved children, those in their homes during this time, if you obey my instructions, I will send legions of my holy angels to protect you.</u>

Do not fear. Throughout the Earth, as all electronics cease,<u> you will have nowhere to turn but to me,</u> the true and only God of endless ages. Pray without ceasing. Pray in the Spirit, trust in me. And I will carry you through. Please be aware <u>that during this time, the resurrection of the dead will take place as the graves of the righteous dead will explode around the entire globe. Simultaneously during this time, many but not all of my living Saints will be transformed by my power and majesty.</u> My children<u> who know me as their Lord and Savior but who are living in sin and willful disobedience will be left behind.</u> That choice is up to them. So, the option is to either obey God now or disobey and be left behind. My beloved children, you asked me why I would allow such a time as this? If you have studied my holy word, you would understand why I will do this. My beautiful Earth has become polluted not so much by man-made chemical emissions, but rather, <u>my Earth has been totally polluted by the filth and degradation of humanity's sins: By the sins of humanity. Sin is destroying humanity, and my Earth is suffering also. So I'm bringing an end to humankind's rule on the planet,</u> down through <u>the six thousand years</u> since I created your planet until now. <u>My created human beings have been hell-bent on making bad choices called sins.</u> These sins are now destroying my Earth. Therefore, I am going to intervene personally.

I will soon implement my plan, <u>which will save humanity from total destruction</u>; since my word says for the elect's sake, <u>I will cut the day short.</u> Also, my intervention will save my Earth. I love my creation, and my plan for the planet which I have created is yet to be fulfilled.

After all, is said and done,<u> my Earth will be given another thousand years in which the glory and beauty will not only be restored but will be</u> multiplied <u>as my Saints rule with me for a thousand years.</u> Read my word, dear ones. Read my scriptures, and I will give you understanding. Trust me my beloved children. I will never leave or forsake you. I will be near to each one of my people who call on me, <u>for I am a God of perfect love, mercy, and grace.</u> I am <u>Yeshua Christ,</u> the Lord.

<u>End of God's message</u>

## SIXTH SEAL) Cosmic Disturbances:

Many things begin to happen near mid-tribulation. First, the capture of Israel/Jerusalem triggers placing the Antichrist's Abomination of desolation in the rebuilt Temple. Second, Nibiru shows up on the scene to block the sun's light from shining on the earth and the moon [period of darkness preceding Rapture]. <u>Third, the proximity of the alien planet crossing the ecliptic causes an earthquake that scripturally makes the mountains and islands move</u>. Finally, the stars of heaven falling to earth are synonymous with God's angels coming to pick up the Raptured. The receding scroll is the feeling received by the Raptured as the angels bring them to heaven: ref Pastor Carl Gallup's Rapture Dream.

## Nibiru

Revelation 8:8 Then the second angel sounded: *Something* like a great **mountain** burning with fire was thrown into the sea, and a third of the sea became blood.

In exploring whether any information supported such a premise, the answer was: Yes

Relative size of Earth and Nibiru Solar System
(Not to scale)

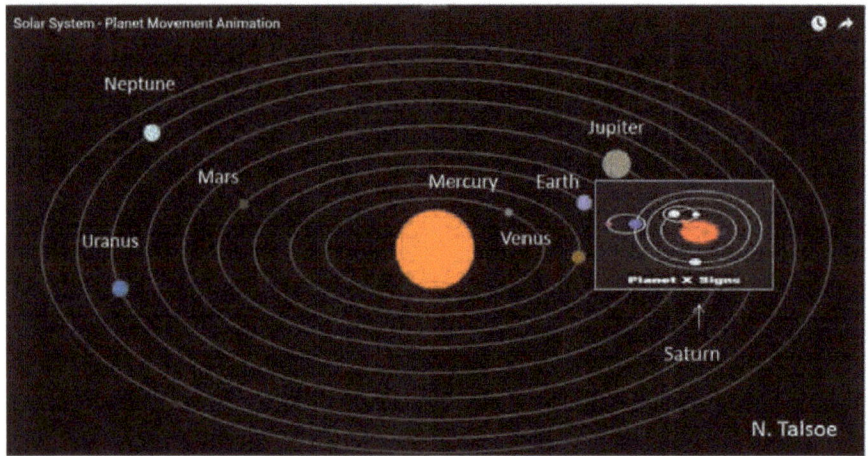

Nibiru planetary system

From Sumerian mythology comes a story of God (mysterious extraterrestrials from "Chariots of the Gods" – von Dannikian) arriving from the heavens to the earth. Sumerian mythology also describes the destroying planet Nibiru as threatening the earth's survival. A Biblical explanation would suggest that these so-called alien gods were fallen angels that God kicked out of heaven. As the sons of man multiplied and produced families, these angels found they lusted for their women, who they considered exquisite and desirable. Their passion for the women caused them to mate with earth's women providing giants in those days called the Nephilim. Goliath was one of those giants who were still around after the flood. One could assume, as former Angels, they were privy to many of heaven's secrets and further think they used that knowledge to do many wondrous things, including genetically altering humanity to be part human and animal. This assumption would account for the many strange images of the early Egyptian empires: part animal, human bodies with bird heads, etc. God finally could take no more and created the flood that destroyed the entire population except for the eight in Noah's family. The book of Enoch and the Bible describes these events.

Is there any doubt that humanity is rapidly approaching the sinfulness threshold that caused God to wipe out the Nephilim and its progeny because it had so contaminated the DNA of humankind?

*Did you know scientists are creating cow/human hybrids, pig/human hybrids, and even mouse/human hybrids? This activity happens daily in labs worldwide, but most people have never even heard of it.* However, human-animal hybrids are a subject of interest today.

The above discussion point is that humanity is always willing to believe that other terrestrials in the universe created us but not our God. God, in Noah's day, sent humanity a Biblical message in destroying humankind with a deluge. Next time He will do so with fire (2 Peter 3:7). Assuming the news of Nibiru and its solar system is correct, only God knows when it will strike. I believe the Biblical earthquakes will give clues to when. The projections were already wrong in previous forecasts between 2003, 2008, and 2012. Satan is delivering the information, and since he is the master of deceit, it is to his advantage to push false information and cause humanity to "cry wolf" before the real thing comes. Presuming that the Sumerian Alien Creator was our Biblical God is heresy. The Bible describes a different story in Genesis 6. The so-called gods from outer space were nothing more than the fallen angels kicked out of heaven by God -- they became the evil giants. God created the universe and all Life, including Lucifer and his fallen angels. What landed on Earth was Satan and his demons – not astronauts.

Since the late 1700s, there has been a history of looking for a ninth planet in our solar system; that would account for the eccentric orbits exhibited by Uranus and Neptune. There is an ongoing debate about whether such a probability lies in our future, which I will cover later. Two pieces of Scripture plus history seem to tie a small brown dwarf solar system with three planets and two moons into a likelihood that it could be the earth's Nemesis. The ancient Sumerian culture named the brown dwarf sun by that name. Whether this small solar system exists or not, its presumption seems to be the best fit for the suffering described on the earth.

Sumerian writings define a small solar system where the sun named Nemesis, with its planets, would orbit the earth's sun every 3600 years. Its orbit is a relative 30 degrees inclination to our solar system's ecliptic. Protagonists claim that the brown dwarf and its planets hide behind our sun. They show spectacular photographs of dual suns that suggest it is close to entering our solar system. Antagonists suggest the opposite, declaring that it does not exist. However, if true, the second half will be much worse with massive Earth changes triggered by earthquakes and volcanic activity that will cause a shift of the earth's mantle around its core. Polar regions will rotate to the equator, and temperate areas will become the North and South poles. Also, *"something* like a great mountain burning with fire was thrown into the sea, " resulting in massive tsunamis a mile high or more. The earth's population will be far less than it is now.

Do the descriptions sound familiar? Are we not now seeing all this happening? Many persecuted Christians are now dying and will continue to die for _not_ embracing the Christian beliefs and religion of God and Jesus Christ. The Antichrist has the beheadings already taking place. A Preterist viewpoint may say that all this occurred in the past: as it did in 70AD, but it is untrue – it will be the future – read Daniel.

Nevertheless, since only 34% of the populace believes in Christianity, most will not. During the 6000-year week, it will be like the game, as mentioned earlier, of chess between Satan and God. They will be the players trying to convince the chess pieces, us, to move according to their biddings. It will be a battle for souls: winners will go to heaven, losers to Hades. Meanwhile, humanity suffers death throughout those 6000 years of waiting for Christ's eternal life in the millennium.

These judgments will occur during Daniel's 7-year timeline, defining the last years of God's week. However, his prophecy, made almost 2600 years ago, only completed 483 years of punishment before being cut short by Christ's crucifixion. His crucifixion marked the transition from the rule of law to the gospel of Jesus Christ in the New Testament. It also left the remaining seven years to be completed sometime in the future. God dispersed the Jews throughout the nations for nearly 2000 years as a punishment for disobeying God. However, He promises the future revival of Israel, as prophesized in:

> **Ezekiel 36:22-24**—"It is not for your sake, O house of Israel, that I am about to act, but for My holy name'… For *I will take you from the nations, gather you from all the lands, and bring you into your land.*"

Only when Ezekiel's promise came true would God re-create Israel as a nation. Only then could "Daniel's timeline" the last week of seven years be finished. At the end of that time, Christ would return in final retribution.

A small solar system with a dwarf sun having a planet, Nibiru, many times the size of our earth, and two others orbiting around it, soon will be in a close encounter with our world. Evidence is already in the sky showing two apparent suns under certain conditions. The second sun is an alien planet within our system that reflects our sun's light. One only must google "two suns" to see the myriad photos and videos showing something there.

Conspiracy allegations suggest that Someone photoshopped the dual sun videos. However, such objections cannot explain how our sun reflecting on a tin roof going east to west was followed 4 hours later similarly by a bright object going west to east. It was pock-marked and rotating under a filtered background. I doubt anyone would spend the time and effort to construct the number of videos available falsely.

Biblical Scripture supports the theory by defining two powerful earthquakes in the end-times 3.5 years apart. The first would occur during the Celestial Display of Seal 6 when the Nibiru System first enters our ecliptic, and (Rev 6:6) "every mountain and island was moved out of its place."

The Second coincidentally would happen when Nibiru is in even closer proximity. With Christ's return at Armageddon 3.5 years later (Rev 16:18,20). "There was a great earthquake, such a mighty and great earthquake as had not occurred since men were on the earth." Then every island fled away, and the mountains were not found.

The first earthquake at mid-trib only moved the mountains and islands while the final quake flattened them, while all the islands disappeared. This "wrecking ball" planet travels its thirty-six hundred years elliptical orbit around our sun, intercepting our ecliptic plane as it arrives and exits closer than when it entered, leaving havoc. According to ancient Sumerian mythology, it has an alleged history, calling it the "destroyer."

While you may dismiss Nibiru as a conspiracy theory that allows a cause-and-effect analysis, it also is a prophesied Biblical event. It will happen whether Nibiru causes it or not. An engineer looking for a statistical correlation between Biblical events and seeing evidence of giant orbs in the sky, believable or not, gives a high probability of how God will handle the punishment. Conspiracy claims notwithstanding, if it looks like a duck and you can see it, I choose to believe my eyes. Besides, He tells what He will do in His dictation to Linda Courtney, and other prophetic ministries have noted Nibiru.

(Revelation 6) Seal 6 [12] I looked when He opened the sixth Seal, and [g]behold, there was a great earthquake, and the sun became black as sackcloth of hair, and the [h] moon became like blood. [13] And the stars of heaven fell to the earth, as a fig tree drops its late figs when it is shaken by a mighty wind. [14] Then the sky [i]receded as a scroll when rolled up, and every mountain and island was moved out of its place. [15] And the kings of the earth, the great men, [j]the rich men, the commanders, the mighty men, every enslaved person, and every free man, hid in the caves and the rocks of the mountains, [16] and said to the mountains and rocks, "Fall on us and hide us from the face of Him who sits on the throne and from the wrath of the Lamb! [17] For the great day of His wrath has come, and who is able to stand?"

In summary:

- Antichrist takes Israel/Jerusalem

- Antichrist sets up the Abomination of desolation Image

- Mark of the Beast implemented [Seal 5]

- Nibiru shows up, causing massive earthquakes and creating darkness of the sun/moon,

- Three days of darkness preceding the Rapture

- Rapture occurs

    (Isaiah 13:10) [10]For the stars of heaven and their constellations Will not give their light; The Sun will be darkened in its going forth, And the moon will not cause its light to shine.

    (Isaiah 13:13) Therefore I will shake the heavens, And the earth will move out of her place, In the wrath of the Lord of hosts And in the day of His fierce anger.

## WORLDS IN COLLISION COMPARISON

Yet to come are the Trumpet and Bowl judgments. These punishments fall within the wrath of God period, aka The Great Tribulation: "there will be suffering as has not been since the beginning of the world until this time, no, nor ever shall be." It will be the last 3.5 years of the seven years. And will include significant earthquakes, Tsunamis, volcanic activities, Earth moving out of its orbit, plagues, nuclear war, pole shift, contaminated lakes and oceans, asteroid contacts, invasion of monsters from the bottomless pit, hurricane winds, scorching heat, and extended darkness. Loss of life would probably be higher than 6 billion people.

The future Trumpet and Bowl punishments exhibit similarities to the God-given plagues against the Egyptian Pharaoh during the Jewish Exodus. The following narrative will cover the period from the 6th Seal in Revelation 6:12, during Mid-Tribulation, to the end of Christ's return. It will begin with the celestial display in Revelation 6 and progress through the Gog-Magog war, followed by the end of God's week with the arrival of Christ at Armageddon on the last fantastic Day of the LORD. The close correlation between Exodus plagues again reinforces that Nibiru was a repeating cycle of the suggested 3600-year elliptical path of this small solar system

Drawing from cultural and cosmological history from around our planet and solar system, Immanuel Velikovsky, in his 1967 book, Worlds in Collision, chronicles support for the existence of Nibiru. He has endeavored to show that a series of cosmic catastrophes occurred as little as 2600 to 3400 years ago throughout stellar history. The warning is that if these things can happen in the past, they may also repeat in the future. His research covered numerous books of antiquity, searching for repeating patterns of destruction. As will be seen, the correlation between these events and the Bible in that time frame is remarkable. Following is a summary of some history from his book compared to related scripture:

Book:

A celestial body that had become a solar system member shortly before – a new comet came very close to Earth. The comet was on its way from its perihelion and touched the Earth with its gaseous tail. One of the first visible signs of this encounter was the Earth's surface reddening with a fine dust of rusty pigment. This stain in the sea, lakes, and rivers *gave a bloody coloring to the water* – the world turned red. Page 64.

Bible:

> (Rev 16:2) the sea became blood as of a dead man, and every living creature in the sea died. (Rev 16:4) [4]....*the rivers and springs of water, and **they became blood**.*

Book:

The ***skin of men and animals was irritated*** by the dust that caused boils, sickness, and cattle death. Page 64-65.

Bible:

> (Rev 16:2) foul and ***loathsome sore*** came upon the men who had the mark of the Beast and those who worshiped his image.

Book:

The Earth entered deeper into the tail of the onrushing comet and approached its body. This engulfment was followed <u>by a disturbance of the rotation of the Earth</u>. Terrific hurricanes swept the Earth because of the change or reversal of the angular velocity of the rotation and because of the sweeping gasses, dust, and cinders of the comet. <u>An exceedingly strong wind endured for seven days</u>. All the time, <u>the land was shrouded in darkness.</u> On the fourth, fifth, and sixth days, the darkness was so dense that the people of Egypt could not stir from their place. Nothing could be discerned. None could speak or hear, nor could anyone venture to take food but laid themselves down – their outward senses in a trance. Thus, they remained overwhelmed by the affliction. *<u>During the plague of darkness, the vast majority of the Israelites perished</u>*. Pg 74.

Bible:

> (Rev 16: 10) [10] … and *<u>his kingdom became full of **darkness**,</u>* and they gnawed their tongues because of the pain.

Book:

The *<u>area of the **earthquake was the entire globe**</u>*. The towns are destroyed --- "all ruined." The hail killed those fleeing from the earthquake, and those that sought shelter from the hail were destroyed by the earthquake. Pg 78-79.

The rush of the atmosphere resulting from inertia when the Earth stopped rotating or shifted its poles contributed to <u>hurricanes of enormous velocity and force of worldwide dimensions</u>. The face of the Earth changed, <u>mountains collapsed,</u> and others <u>grew and rose over the onrushing waters driven from the Ocean's basin.</u> Pg 82.

Bible:

> (Rev 16:18-21) There was *<u>a **great earthquake**, such a mighty and great earthquake as had not occurred since men were on the Earth.</u>* [20]Then, every island fled away,

and the mountains were not found. [21]And great hail from Heaven fell upon men, each hailstone about the weight of a talent. Men blasphemed God because of the plague of the hail since that plague was exceedingly great.

Are not these previous catastrophes similar to those covered by the Bible in the Seal, Trumpet, and Bowl judgments? In both cases, a "wrecking ball" planet from outer space could cause them.

## RAPTURE: Christ in the clouds

Zecharaiah 14:5 tells us, Thus the Lord my God will come, And all the saints with Him.

(Matthew 24:29-31) The Coming of the Son of Man [29] "Immediately after the tribulation of those days the sun will be darkened, and the moon will not give its light; the stars will fall from heaven, [Comment: stars are God's angels that collect the Raptured].

The above tells us that immediately after the early tribulation of the first five Seals, Nibiru shows up in our ecliptic plane to darken our earth, moon, and sun. Thus, it begins the days of darkness God warns us about in His story for Linda Courtney to record. Our Father then explains to us metaphorically that when the "fig tree's" branches start to blossom, we know that summer is near: i.e., we perceive the season of our Lord's return.

(**Matt 24:32-35**), God also pictures the season from

[32] "Now learn this parable from the fig tree: When its branch has already become tender and puts forth leaves, you know that summer *is* near. [33] So you also, when you see all these things, know that [c]it is near—at the doors! [34] Assuredly, I say to you, *this generation [70-80 years from the rebirth of Israel] will by no means pass away till all these things take place.* [35] Heaven and earth will pass away, but My words will by no means pass away.

(1 Thessalonians 4:13-18) And <u>the dead in Christ will rise first.</u> <u>[17]</u>Then <u>we who are alive and remain shall be caught up together with them in the clouds to meet the Lord in the air. And thus, we shall always be with the Lord.</u>

The previous scripture appears to address all the souls since the crucifixion of Christ. They would be the harvest from God's planting His seeds during those 2000+ years.

(1 Corinthians 15:52) in a moment, in the twinkling of an eye, at the last Trumpet. For the Trumpet will sound, and the dead will be raised incorruptible, and we shall be changed.

While the word Rapture does not appear in the Bible, clearly, the event shows in verse Matthew 24:31. "***the angels were gathering His elect from the four winds***, from one end of heaven to the other. Christ does not make a return to earth at this time.

The scripture talks about the sun and moon's presumed impossible simultaneous eclipse. A sun eclipse requires the moon is between the sun and the earth: a moon eclipse requires our world is between the moon and the sun. To simultaneously eclipse, the sun and moon need a sizeable celestial mass between the sun and our planet and moon, i.e., Nibiru. Nemesis is estimated to be 50x more massive than our world, while Nibiru is close to 5x in size. Any planet more massive than our moon would make the eclipse more prolonged and darker because of its size. It would eliminate the sun's corona and the stars that would otherwise shine in the black sky next to the sun. The darkness, indeed, would be stifling. ***<u>A simultaneous darkened sun and red or dark moon is impossible without an intruding alien planet eclipsing the sun and the earth.</u>*** **It would** appear <u>*during the celestial display, referred to in Seal* </u>six,

(Isaiah 13:13): [13] And the earth will move out of her place

(Revelation 6:14) every mountain and island will move out of its place.

Our moon must be in our planet's shadow on the other side, while our planet would be in the shade of *the different alien world between us and the sun*. So it could only be one of the Nemesis/Nibiru planets that, *if large enough,* will entirely block out the sun from reflecting on us or the moon.

God's goal always has been for humanity to believe the Gospel of Jesus Christ. It would be unlike Him to punish further His elect if they had already met the criteria for salvation. Hence, the Rapture of the elect before the last 3.5 brutal years would make great sense and satisfy the scripture referring to a shortened Tribulation for "Born again" Christians. In this view: God chooses His elect, during the first 3.5 years, rather than having them remain with the unbelievers the entire duration to taste God's wrath. The following scriptures validate that God does not want his "born again" going through the Great Tribulation. So, believers will Rapture from our world before the Wrath of GOD.

> (2 Peter 2:4-9): [4] For if God did not spare the angels who sinned, but cast them down to hell and delivered them into chains of darkness, to be reserved for judgment;[5] and did not spare the ancient world, but saved Noah, one of eight people, a preacher of righteousness, bringing in the flood on the world of the ungodly;[6] and turning the cities of Sodom and Gomorrah into ashes, condemned them to destruction, making them an example to those who afterward would live ungodlily; [7] and delivered righteous Lot, who was oppressed by the filthy conduct of the wicked [8] (for that righteous man, dwelling among them, tormented his righteous soul from day to day by seeing and hearing their lawless deeds)— [9] then the Lord knows how to deliver the godly out of temptations and to reserve the unjust under punishment for the day of judgment,

> 1 Thessalonians 1:10, [10] and to wait for His Son from heaven, whom He raised from the dead, even Jesus who delivers us from the wrath to come.

> (1 Thessalonians 5:9) [9] For God did not appoint us to wrath, but to obtain salvation through our Lord Jesus Christ,

(Romans 5:8-9) ²Much more then, having now been justified by His blood, we shall be saved from wrath through Him

(Revelation 3:10) I also will keep you from the hour of trial

These scriptures prove that we are saved from God's wrath to come. The worthy "left behind" survivors that endured the Great Tribulation testament of fire by surviving to pass through, persevere, and join Christ as his priests and kings to serve Him in His one-thousand-year reign.

## WRATH OF GOD (2nd 3.5 years) Antichrist in control

Daniel's Timeline initiating this narrative places the Wrath of GOD punishments at mid-tribulation after the Wrath of the Lamb. Thus, the Antichrist, owning the Temple Mount, discontinues the first 3.5 years of allowed sacrifice to set his Abomination Idol up in God's Sanctuary for the final 3.5-years. In the second half of the tribulation, a new truth becomes apparent: God's two Witnesses will Tread the Holy City For the Final 3.5 years. The Abomination of Desolation Idol is in place for the same duration. We know that the witnesses' death and resurrection will occur at the end of the 42-month or 1260 days period. Thus, they will have finished God's assigned task of giving testimony and prophesying for Him. His witnesses will have the power to cause drought during their days of prophecy, turn water to blood, and cause plagues on the enemy as often as desired. However, to show His Glory, God will permit the Antichrist to arise from the bottomless pit and kill the witnesses, leaving them to lie on the street for three-and-a-half days. It will happen in full view of those still on earth who celebrate the sight. Then, after three-and-a-half days, God will breathe life back into them, saying "come up here" in a loud voice, causing great fear in all those watching. Their death and resurrection must happen within the last 3.5 days of the end period. It is because the timing of Revelation 11:13 calls out an earthquake during their revival that coincides with the same hour as the quake in Revelation 16:18, Bowl 7; i.e., the one that was "so great it had never happened before." So, if Trumpet 7 coincides with Bowl 7, then Bowl 1-7 must also happen on that last day: The Day of the LORD. Therefore, the

## Wrath of God

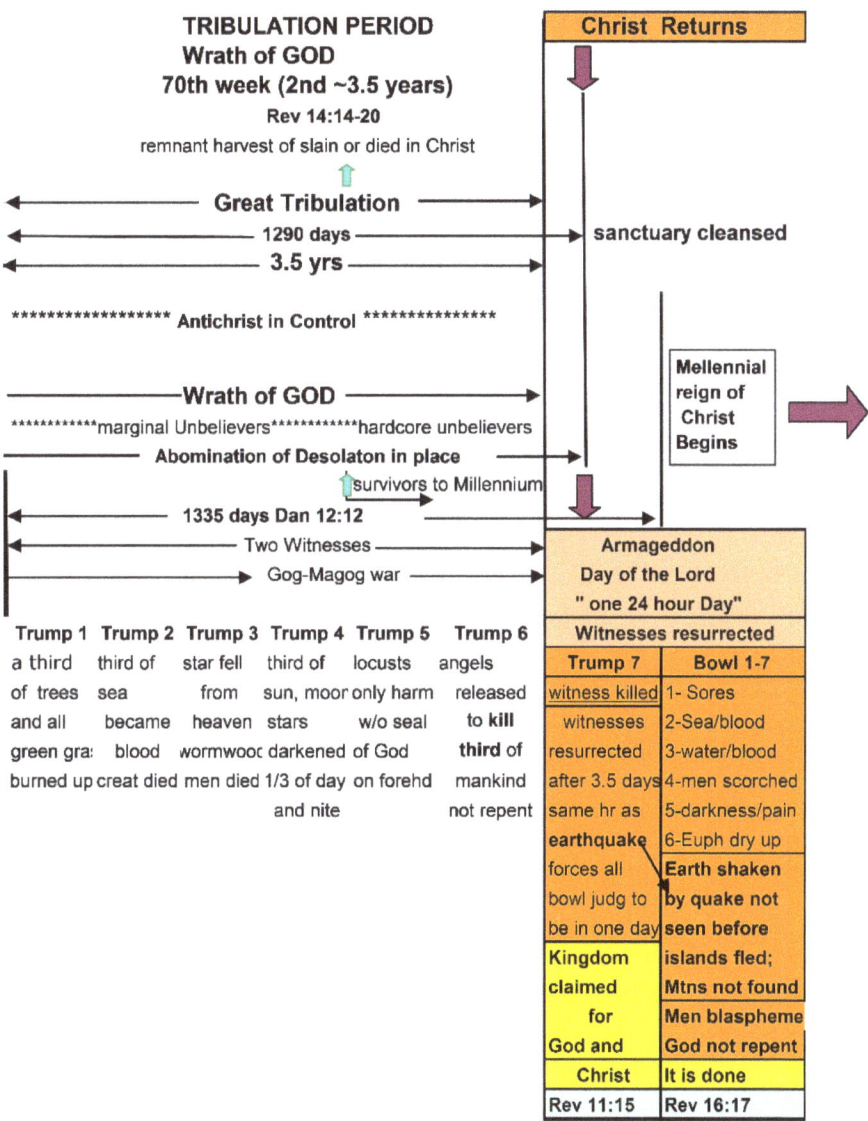

**TRIBULATION PERIOD**
**Wrath of GOD**
**70th week (2nd ~3.5 years)**
Rev 14:14-20
remnant harvest of slain or died in Christ

Christ Returns

Great Tribulation

1290 days ———— sanctuary cleansed

3.5 yrs

****************** Antichrist in Control ***************

————————Wrath of GOD ————————

************marginal Unbelievers************hardcore unbelievers

Abomination of Desolaton in place

survivors to Millennium

Mellennial reign of Christ Begins

1335 days Dan 12:12

Two Witnesses

Gog-Magog war

Armageddon
Day of the Lord
" one 24 hour Day"

Witnesses resurrected

| Trump 1 | Trump 2 | Trump 3 | Trump 4 | Trump 5 | Trump 6 | Trump 7 | Bowl 1-7 |
|---------|---------|---------|---------|---------|---------|---------|----------|
| a third | third of | star fell | third of | locusts | angels | witness killed | 1- Sores |
| of trees | sea | from | sun, moor | only harm | released | witnesses | 2-Sea/blood |
| and all | became | heaven | stars | w/o seal | to **kill** | resurrected | 3-water/blood |
| green gra: | blood | wormwooc | darkened | of God | **third** of | after 3.5 days | 4-men scorched |
| burned up | creat died | men died | 1/3 of day | on forehd | mankind | same hr as | 5-darkness/pain |
| | | | and nite | | not repent | earthquake | 6-Euph dry up |
| | | | | | | forces all | Earth shaken |
| | | | | | | bowl judg to | by quake not |
| | | | | | | be in one day | seen before |
| | | | | | | Kingdom | islands fled; |
| | | | | | | claimed | Mtns not found |
| | | | | | | for | Men blaspheme |
| | | | | | | God and | God not repent |
| | | | | | | Christ | It is done |
| | | | | | | Rev 11:15 | Rev 16:17 |

# 2ND JUDGING: CHRIST JUDGES THE NATIONS

Who?                        The Nations from the Rapture to Armageddon
Good/Bad Metaphor: Sheep vs. Goats
Period covered:         from Rapture until 1 day short of last 3.5 years
Salvation criteria:      "Random acts of goodness."
War:                         Gog-Magog ending in Armageddon

### God incarnate as Christ lands on/ Splits Mount Olivet

Once Jesus has delivered those Raptured to heaven, the scriptural task changes. The term LORD, my God, tells us that while we may see Christ land on and split the Mount of Olives, God's personality is in charge.

(Zechariah 14) ³Then the LORD will go forth And fight against those nations, [Comment: Those He aided in punishing Israel] As He fights in the day of battle. thus ⁵the LORD my God will come, And all the saints with HIm.

All thirty-six references in the Bible recognize the term using capital letters for LORD as Father GOD. Thus, the Saints just delivered to heaven would join God in His battle with souls already there. True to His word, God manifests as Christ to pick up the fight with Gog-Magog, the latest beast, the future neo-Ottoman Caliphate. He had just finished aiding in punishing Israel. As the final battle approaches, this six-nation Beast will grow to ten and perhaps more additional countries.

# TRUMPET/BOWL JUDGMENTS

Because the numerous timing coincidences and interaction events between the Trumpet and Bowl judgments set the stage for everything else that happens, it is necessary to define that relationship upfront. Analyzing the Trumpet and Bowl judgments show that:

7th Trumpet

> (Rev11:13) [13] In the same hour [Comment: as the 2 witnesses resurrection], there was a great earthquake, and a tenth of the city fell.

and 7th Bowl

> (Rev 16:17) [17] Then the seventh angel poured out his bowl into the air, and a loud voice came out of the temple of heaven, from the throne, saying, "It is done!" [18] And there were noises and thunderings and lightnings; and there was a great earthquake, such a mighty and great earthquake as had not occurred since men were on the earth.

The above two witness resurrection happens simultaneously [with the battle of Armageddon and the most horrendous earthquake that ever happened].

The great earthquake in Trump 7 explains that:

> [12] And they heard a loud voice from heaven saying to them, "Come up here." And they [Comment: two witnesses] ascended to heaven in a cloud, and their enemies saw them. [13] In the same hour there was a great earthquake).

This period would place their final day as the Awesome Day of the LORD, the day of Christ's return. The massive earthquake of Bowl 7 would be the same as in Trump 7 Rev 11:13. Therefore, God's resurrection of the two witnesses coincides with Christ's coming.

In the Bible, the Trumpet judgments sequentially precede the Bowl punishments tending to make readers believe they are chronological. However, they are not. The Trumpet judgments will occur incrementally over the last 3.5 years, while the Bowl judgments coincide with the 7th Trumpet on the final day of the age. In general, this allows comparing the worst it gets with the increased severity of punishment. For example, the most straightforward correlation shows that Trumpet 1 and Bowl 1 relate sores on sinners due to earlier trees and grass burning. Trumpet 2 increased from 1/3 of the sea, turning to blood to the whole sea, becoming blood in Bowl 2.

| Trumpet 1-trees and grass burn | Bowl 1 – sores on sinners |
| Trumpet 2- 1/3 sea became blood | Bowl 2—Sea became blood |
| Trumpet 3- Waters, Rivers struck | Bowl 3—waters, rivers > blood |
| Trumpet 4- sun struck | Bowl 4—sun-scorched men |
| Trumpet 5-Locusts from the pit | Bowl 5 – Men in pain |
| Trumpet 6- Euphrates angels kill .3 | Bowl 6—the Euphrates dries up |
| Trumpet 7- Kingdom of our Lord | Bowl 7 – It is done |

All the above judgments will concurrently build to the final battle between Christ and Satan.

**Beast Evolution**

The evolution of the beast has been brewing ever since Adam and Eve. First, God chose Israel and the Jews as His people and then spent 6000 years collecting all the souls He could. The deciding tenet was that if you believed in and obeyed God, you were good: If not, you were evil. Those that did not believe in God worshipped idols, the sun, or other mythical characters made up by humankind driven by power and a desire for control.

**The Beast from the Sea**

(Revelation 13) Then I stood on the sand of the sea. And I saw a beast rising out of the sea, having [b]seven heads and ten horns, and on his horns ten crowns, and on his heads a blasphemous name. [2] Now the beast which I saw was like a leopard, his feet were like the feet of a bear *[Iran,*

*Persia],* and his mouth like the mouth of <u>a lion</u> *[Babylon]. The dragon [Turkey]* gave him his power, throne, and great authority.

It would have been the Grecian dynasty of Alexander the Great circa 330–164 BCE before his death. A brutal general, Antiochus of Alexander's army, picked up the pieces of the Seleucid Kingdom containing [Greece, Turkey, Syria, and Egypt]. The latter date of 167 BCE would have happened after the breakup of Alexander the Great.

³ And I saw one of his heads <u>*[Ottoman Empire]* as if it had been mortally wounded,</u> and his deadly wound was healed *[to become the neo-Ottoman Caliphate].* And all the world marveled and followed the beast. ⁴ So they worshiped the dragon [Turkey, Iran, Syria, Lebanon –10 country beast] who gave authority to the beast; and they worshiped the beast, saying, "Who is like the beast? Who is able to make war with him?"

The sequence of empires taken from TIME MAPS

https://www.timemaps.com/history/middle-east-1500bc/

> (Revelation 17:8-14) ⁸ The beast that you saw was, and is not, and will ascend out of the bottomless pit and go to perdition. And those who dwell on the earth will marvel, whose names <u>are not</u> written in the Book of Life from the foundation of the world when they see the beast that was and is not, and yet is.¹⁰ There are: (a). Also, seven kings. (b) Five have fallen, (c) one is, and the other has not yet come. (d) And when he comes, he must continue a short time. ¹¹ The beast that was, and is not, is himself also the eighth, and is of the seven, and is going to ⁽ᶠ⁾ perdition. ¹² "<u>The ten horns which you saw are ten kings who have received no kingdom as yet</u>, but they receive authority for one hour as kings with the beast. ¹³ These are of one mind, and they will give their power and authority to the beast. ¹⁴ These will make war with the Lamb, and the Lamb will overcome them, for He is Lord of lords and King of kings; and those who are with Him are called, chosen, and faithful."

The listed dates showed when that empire defeated its predecessor in the number sequence.

Number four, below, lists the countries that define the beast from the sea in 175-164 BCE as Greek General Antiochus IV Epiphanes. It has a Leopard body _representing Greece,_ a lion's mouth, and a bear's paws.

This description is the one John saw when he wrote the prophecy in Revelation 13, almost 260 years later. It indicates that the 168 BCE beast is identical to the one prophesied for the end-times.

The first beast, Syria, King of the North, has grown through territory acquisition during the back and forth battles between the Seleucid and Ptolemaic dynasties. It has now morphed into the new King of the North: Gog-Magog. Moreover, Daniel 11:40-45 suggests that those verses jump into the future to define the latest version of the Not-yet-come monster, the Neo-Ottoman Empire. It is about to replicate itself from the blueprint left by Antiochus IV as we enter the end-time just before the return of our Lord Jesus Christ. (2)

### Who is the 2022+ Beast?

Number 8, below the new neo-Ottoman Caliphate, was the Beast that has "not yet come" until 1917. It had outlasted the previous beasts: Assyria, Babylonia, Medio-Persia, Alexander the Great's Greek Empire, and Rome until they allied with Germany in WW1 and lost to become the Beast who is not: by becoming individual nations: by fragmenting themselves out of existence.

### Is the Antichrist Muslim?

The Tribulation will begin with a promise of peace from the Antichrist and church members departing God. The two scriptures that tell us are:

> (Daniel 9:27) [27]Then he [Antichrist] shall confirm a covenant with many for one week [comment: 7 years]; But in the middle of the week, He shall bring an end to sacrifice and offering. And on the wing of abominations

shall be one who makes desolate, Even until the consummation, which is determined, Is poured out on the desolate."

(2 Thessalonians 2:3-4)  ³Let no one deceive you by any means; for that Day [comment: return of Christ] will not come unless the falling away comes first, and the man of sin is revealed, the son of perdition, ⁴who opposes and exalts himself above all that is called God or that is worshiped, so that he sits as God[c] in the temple of God, showing himself that he is God.

Also, recall earlier that in Daniel 9:26, scripture tells us that: And *__the people of the prince  [Antichrist] who is to come__* Shall destroy the city and the sanctuary.

**Of the seven kings: Below first Five have fallen**,

1. Assyria-Syria **722** BCE
2. Babylonia, (Iraq) **586** BCE LION
3. Medio-Persia (Iran) **539** BCE BEAR
4. Greece: Seleucid Kingdom/Ptolemaic Turkey, Syria, and Egypt **330–164** BCE. Antiochus **rule 175-164 BCE**: Died in 164 BCE. Zeus Desecration of the second Temple by Antiochus IV Epiphanes in **168** BCE. Participating countries are **Syria, Iraq, Iran, Turkey, Greece, Egypt, Libya, Ethiopia/Cush, Sudan, and Lebanon**
5. Rome **100** BCE-750 AD
   **One is:**
6. ***Original Ottoman Empire (637-1914)*** LEOPARD
a. [Seleucid Kingdom (4 generals) Syria, Turkey, Greece/Macedonia, Egypt] **Is not:**
7. Original Ottoman Empire **dismantled** in ***1917 WW1***
   **Not yet come:**
8. **(New neo-Ottoman Empire).**
   Includes (Syria, Iraq, Iran), (Turkey, Egypt) (Libya, Ethiopia/Cush), and other *guesses* 2018-2028, Greece, Lebanon, and Sudan

What quickly becomes apparent is that no matter which definition one selects, the **first Five have fallen, One is, Is not, and Not yet come,** the nations of the beast, over time, have been the same. Therefore, specific interest categories are: *First five*, *One is*, *is not*, and *Not Yet come.*

It quickly becomes apparent that no matter which definition one selects, the **first Five have fallen; one is, Is not, and Not yet come;** they are all Islamic.

The above shows that Satan has not changed his stripes – although the various countries may have changed their name over time, they predominantly hate the Jews. That is not to say one can paint the country with a broad brush by inferring there are no Christians in each of them; God calls to all of us. However, where there are many Radical Islamists, Christians and Jews will be persecuted by those who hate them.

Number four, above, lists the countries defining the beast from the sea in 175-164 BCE as Antiochus IV Epiphanes. It has a Leopard body, a lion's mouth, and a bear's paws. This description is the same one John saw when he wrote the prophecy in Revelation 13 almost 260 years later.

It indicates that the 168 BCE beast is identical to the one prophesied for the end-times. The first beast, Syria, who was King of the North, has grown through territory acquisition during the back and forth battles between the *Seleucid* and *Ptolemaic dynasties.* It has now morphed into the new King of the North: Gog-Magog. Moreover, Daniel 11:40-45 suggests that those verses jump into the future to define the latest version of the Not-yet-come monster, the Neo-Ottoman Empire. It is about to replicate itself from the blueprint left by Antiochus IV as we enter the end-time just before the return of our Lord Jesus Christ.

Even worse for the Arab countries, the signed termination at midnight on 14 May 1948 of the British Mandate, with a stroke of a pen, fulfilled Isaiah 66 and created Israel.

> (Isaiah 66:7-8): [7] "Before she was in labor, she gave birth; Before her pain came, She delivered a male child. [8] Who has heard such a thing? Who has seen such things? Shall

the earth be made to give birth in one day? <u>Or shall a nation be born at once?</u> (2)

Israel is the country of God that Islam always intends to destroy, no matter the beast version. So we may be curious to know who is the 2022+ Antichrist. Only one name comes to mind.

## OBAMA the 2022+ Beast

So who will be this man of perdition that will become the Antichrist and resurrect the past Ottoman empire to become its neo-Ottoman replacement? The one who will become the Antichrist, most likely, is already on the scene making disparaging remarks about the Bible and Christianity. If an empathetic populous embraces the evil actions of the Antichrist, widespread Christian persecution will follow. The only thing protecting us from this pending disaster is if people turn to God in prayer, confessing our sinful nature while repenting and asking forgiveness in the name of our Lord Jesus Christ. However, neither history nor the Biblical book of Revelation bodes well for that expectation.

From my perspective, only one name comes to mind: **Barak Obama**. The end-times *signs and wonders* described in the Bible started on the night of Obama's 2012 election win. It was *the mark of the beast, winning lottery number 666.* Of his other remarkable feats:

1. He is the only president I remember that has disparaged the Bible, in this case, talking about the Sermon on the Mount. "Obama Mocks and attacks Jesus Christ and the Bible. A top U.S. evangelical leader accused Sen. Barack Obama of deliberately distorting the Bible and taking a "fruitcake interpretation" of the U.S. Constitution."

2. On YouTube videos, Obama remarked about his Muslim religion before correcting himself with a prod from the host, saying, don't you mean Christian

3. Compelling evidence from a forensic evaluation of his long-form birth certificate indicates it is counterfeit: <u>*He was born*</u>

*in Kenya*. Even a novice like me could see that someone cut and pasted it from another document

4. A Near-Death Experience of a 15-year-old secular Jewish boy told a Jewish Rabbi in Israel; that in heaven, he was told that Obama was the Antichrist and would start World III. Before rejecting the boys, the statement does not the statistics of the statement of a secular 15-year boy who knew nothing of the Bible ring true?

5. In a speech on February 27th to Kristof of The New York Times, Barack Hussein Obama said the "*Muslim call to prayer* " is *one of the prettiest sounds on Earth at sunset.*

6. He supported abortion, gay marriage, and homosexuality against God during his administration.

7. The Bible constantly tells us there will be signs and wonders: the night Obama won the election in 2012, the winning lottery number was 666, the mark of the beast

8. *Obama abstained;* For70 years, the U.N. had annually petitioned their council members to vote for an Israeli partition to bring forth the Palestinian state. Over those seventy years, the *United States always vetoed* the partition vote *until he abstained,* leaving the partitioning vote.

The night the gay marriage law passed, the White House was lit with rainbow LGBT colors that also happened to be around God's throne.

Obama is still here, and we will see him as Antichrist soon.

## The Harlot: City

Revelation 17 tells us that the Beast of seven heads and ten horns reflects seven mountains on which the Harlot sits, and the ten horns are kings that have not yet committed themselves to the Antichrist beast. Further on, Rev 17:18 describes the Harlot as a city that reigns over the kings of the earth. The original Harlot was the City of Babylon, which Saddam

Hussein partially rebuilt in Iraq. So, who is <u>today's</u> Mystery Babylon that will satisfy Revelation 17? While many believe it is the "United States," It is not.

The Fall of Babylon the Great

> (Revelation 18). [2] And he cried mightily with a loud voice, saying, "Babylon the great is fallen, is fallen, and has become a dwelling place of demons, a prison for every foul spirit, and a cage for every unclean and hated bird [4]and God has remembered her iniquities—death and mourning and famine. And she will be utterly burned with fire, for strong is the Lord God who [f]judges her. Standing at a distance **for** fear of her torment, saying, 'Alas, alas, that great city Babylon, that mighty city! **For in one hour, your judgment has come.'**

The World Mourns Babylon's Fall

> [20]"Rejoice over her, O heaven, and you [j]holy apostles and prophets, for God has avenged you on her!"

Finality of Babylon's Fall:

It will have all the earmarks of a nuclear attack: therefore, her plagues "<u>will come</u>" in one day. The tell-all phrase, "<u>will come</u>," proves everything described from this point on has not yet happened.

> (Revelation 18-8) [8] Therefore, her plagues will come in one day—death, mourning, and famine. And she will be utterly burned with fire, for strong *is* the Lord God who [i]judges her.

> (Isaiah 34:5,8-10): [8]<u>For it is the Day of The LORD's vengeance,</u> [9] Its streams <u>shall be</u> turned into pitch, *[tar]* And its dust into brimstone *[sulfur]*; Its land shall become burning pitch [comment: tar]. [10]<u>It shall not be quenched night or day;</u> Its smoke shall ascend forever.

Every shipmaster, all who travel by ship, sailors, and as many as trade on the sea, stood at a distance [18] and cried out when they saw the smoke of her burning, saying, 'What is like this great city?' [11]"And the merchants of the earth will weep and mourn over her,[19] 'Alas, alas, that great city, in which all who had ships on the sea became rich by her wealth! For in one hour, she [i]is made desolate.' [direct hint at the Red Sea Coast]

Ezekiel 25:13 Teman; Dedan shall fall by the sword. [Saudi Arabia towns along Red Sea coast]

The Harlot would die by fire: Revelation 17:1616 And the ten horns [10 kings who will give alliance to the caliphate] which you [a]saw on the beast, these will hate the harlot, make her desolate and naked, eat her flesh and burn her with fire.

Zech 5 describes a "flying scroll" in the land of Shinar between Iran and Iraq that would account for all of the above. Their natural animosity between Iran (Shite) and Arabia (Sunni).

Revelation 18:21 "Thus with violence the great city Babylon shall be thrown down and shall not be found anymore.

The carnage wrought on the Saudi Arabian Peninsula leaves all the oil fields in flames from the cities of the north down to the south, from Seir, Dedan, Mecca to Teman [all in Saudi Arabia]. The devastation would happen in only 60 minutes, leaving smoke seen for miles, invoking a vision of a nuclear holocaust like Sodom and Gomorrah. Furthermore, it would leave the territory uninhabitable for generations. Zion, therefore, warns anyone who lives in Babylon to flee.

This previous analysis identifies Saudi Arabia's Mecca as the new Babylon. The new neo-Ottoman Empire would be complete with the alliance of the surrounding Muslim countries of uncommitted kings who would have reason to <u>hate the Harlot.</u> Why? Because Saudi Arabia would feed the Antichrist's enemies with oil to the detriment of Satan's plans.

Turkey and Iran were natural competitors of Arabia, although one is Sunni and the other is Shite. The fact the Bible says: "Babylon is fallen! Fallen is that great city whose ruins of the old Babylon are still in Iraq; argue that it is yet to happen. The thought would presume that a partially rebuilt Babylon in Iraq would not have enough value for someone to seek to destroy it. Zechariah 5 makes a great case that Iran, the natural enemy of Arabia, will devastate the new Babylon City of Mecca.

Do you know that the Bible identifies In Zechariah 5 a flying scroll that attacks evil? Its flying scroll has dimensions that are valid for a small missile. Its base would be in the land of Shinar, Iraq, and Iran. With a natural animosity between Iran and Arabia and Iran bent on developing missiles, the destruction of Mecca by Iran looks very plausible.

**Beast from the Earth**

The Antichrist and False Prophet will both be human. However, while a <u>symbolic sea beast comprises countries</u> representing the Antichrist, the <u>Beast from the earth</u> will be the last Pontiff: i.e., the False Prophet, who will cause those dwelling on our planet to worship the Antichrist. He also will receive his authority from Satan, represented by the new King of the North: the neo-Ottoman Caliphate, whose deadly wound became healed by ten former beast nations giving allegiance to the new emerging Beast. The nations forming the Biblical Beast from the sea are all Muslims created by an evolution of former empires that, over time, sequentially ruled their respective territories only to become absorbed by the next emerging Empire.

Although the countries were also "beasts," this one will be the last and worst humanity will ever see <u>the end-time 2022+ beast.</u>

On February 4, 2019, at the 'Global Conference on Human Fraternity,' Pope Francis and leading Sunni Imam Sheikh Ahmed al-Tayeb signed a document that targets a "one world religion." His contention is that: we are all children of God but seek Him in different ways giving us all other paths to the same God." The Pope's lie does not agree with the Christian Bible, which states the approach to God is through Jesus Christ. Moreover, such thinking only paves the way for the New World Order, where the Antichrist will reign supreme with the help of the False Prophet. Furthering the notion that Pope Francis is the False Prophet are the following quotes:

- o The Pope said in St Patrick's Cathedral, N.Y. City, "Jesus's life ended in failure on the cross." For this blasphemous statement, the people in the church clapped and praised his deceiving speech.

- o He followed up with the following statement in the Inquisitr magazine: "When we read about Creation in Genesis, we run the risk of imagining God was a magician, with a magic wand able to do everything. But that is not so. He created human beings and let them develop according to the internal laws that he gave to each one so they would reach their fulfillment." i.e., he endorsed the theory of evolution.

- o World Government Must Rule U.S. 'For Their Own Good

- o Speaking with Ecuador's "El Universo" newspaper, the Pope said that the United Nations doesn't have enough power and must be granted complete governmental control "for the good of humanity."

- o The Vatican Calls for New World Economic Order: published October 24, 2011 – Associated Press

Throughout the Pope's papacy, he lays the groundwork for a one-world religion: -- where is the outrage! -- Scarcely anyone seems to care. The Bible, prophesying such conditions for the end-times, admits the majority will embrace the Antichrist. It is starting to happen, reaffirming that we are looking at God's week's end. The Pope already supports Chrislam, a combination of Christianity and Islam. Already 72 churches in the U.S. practice that false religion.

162

(Revelation 13:11-17) [11] Then I saw another beast coming up out of the earth, and he had two horns like a lamb and spoke like a dragon. [12] And he exercises all the authority of the first Beast in his presence and causes the earth and those who dwell in it to worship the first Beast, whose deadly wound was healed. [13] He performs great signs so that he even makes fire come down from heaven on the earth in the sight of men. [14] And he deceives those who dwell on the earth by those signs which he was granted to do in the sight of the Beast, telling those who dwell on the earth to make an image to the Beast who was wounded by the sword and lived. [15] He was granted power to give breath to the image of the Beast, that the image of the Beast should both speak and cause as many as would not worship the image of the Beast to be killed. [16] He causes all, both small and great, rich and poor, free and slave, to receive a mark on their right hand or on their foreheads, [17] and that no one may buy or sell except one who has [a]the mark or the name of the Beast, or the number of his name.

(Revelation 19:20) Then the Beast was captured and with him the false prophet who worked signs in his presence, by which he deceived those who received the mark of the Beast and those who worshiped his image. These two were cast alive into the lake of fire burning with brimstone.

(Matthew 25:31) [The Son of Man Will Judge the Nations] "When the Son of Man comes in His glory, and all the holy angels with Him, then He will sit on the throne of His glory.

# 3RD JUDGING FINAL BATTLE

Who?

| | |
|---|---|
| A remnant evil population: | *The grapes of wrath* |
| Good/Bad Metaphor: | Sweet grapes vs. bitter grapes |
| Period covered: | 1 day, Last day of the 6000-year week |
| Salvation criteria: | none, total retribution |
| War: Armageddon | Christ versus Satan in the final battle |
| Salvation criteria: | none |

Revelation 7 states that John saw a great multitude no one could number from all nations in white robes standing before the throne of the Lamb. Then we read, "These are the ones who come out of the Great Tribulation, washed their robes and made them white in the blood of the Lamb. These would be the sheep sorted from Christ's judgment that would make the millennium.

Coming out of the ***Great Tribulation, the last 3.5 years,*** the robes being made white by the blood of the Lamb could only mean a large number of Satan's followers had found salvation despite being previously followers of the Antichrist. "How could this be?" These minions of Satan must have confessed their sins, repented, and asked for forgiveness in the name of Jesus Christ to justify the purity of their white robes: validation is they will be in heaven. So, what happened? God will happen; He will outsmart Satan by pouring His Holy Spirit on all flesh in Joel 2:28. Suddenly, every one of Satan's followers will become "temples of God" for holding the Holy Spirit. How embarrassing for Satan.

His followers now had another option to consider. With a "multitude, no one could number," Rebelling leaders will embrace the Holy Spirit and

Christ by proselytizing a massive portion of Satan's followers to convert to Christ instead of following Satan. Moreover, these people going through the furnace of affliction would remain alive to populate Christ's millennial reign. It would consist of flesh and blood and resurrected souls. This event should trigger the massive revival expected by the numerous prophetic ministries as humans begin to realize the corruption of their leaders.

## WWIII GOG-MAGOG war starts

The early verses of Zechariah 14 quote from Joel 2, "For the day of the LORD is coming; it is at hand," which means the Last "Day of the LORD" has not happened yet. So Joel 2:2 calls out: A day of darkness and gloominess, and a day of clouds and thick darkness, mimicking Zechariah 14:6 "It shall come to pass in that day That there will be no light, the lights will diminish.

In Ezekiel 5, God explains that Israel must answer for its disobedience, causing Him to help the Beast capture Israel. He then turns against those He helped by going to war against Gog of Magog: The Antichrist He initially assisted. Thus, the last 3.5 years will see the Gog-Magog war morph into Armageddon, the last day of God's week when Christ will return to battle all the nations of the world on the plains of Meggido.

Ezekiel 5 says, "I will gather all the nations [Comment: alluding to the final battle with Satan]," but first, When venting His fury, God states how personally He takes Israel's misconduct in saying, "Indeed I, even I, am against you and will execute judgments in your midst in the sight of the nations."

> (Ezekiel 5:5-10), 'This is Jerusalem; I [Yahweh] have set her in the midst of the nations and the countries all around her. But, because of her disobedience, I will fight against Jerusalem to punish them for rebelling against My judgments and not walking in My statutes nor kept My judgments. [8] therefore thus says the LORD God: 'Indeed I, even I, am against you and will execute judgments

in your midst in the sight of the nations [Comment: surrounding Muslim nations].

### Who is Gog-Magog?

(Daniel 9:26) And the people of the prince who is to come shall destroy the city and the sanctuary. And they did in 70AD. Who were "the people" of this"prince to come?" Contrary to popular belief, they were not Roman Europeans; the "people" were instead Muslim: i.e., Roman Troops conscripted from the surrounding Arab countries. Explicit in that observation, the Antichrist, "Prince," also must be Muslim.

O "Hope of Israel Ministries" gives us the following conclusion: overwhelming evidence from ancient historians defined the ethnicity of "Roman" people who destroyed Jerusalem and the Temple in 70AD as Muslims. Conscripted Roman soldiers came from the local populace of Arabs and Muslims who dominated the region. Syrians, Egyptians, and troops from Asia Minor made up the Roman legions of the Middle East. Thus, the Antichrist is Muslim.

O One of the proofs submitted is from the book, Soldiers, Cities, and Civilians in Roman Syria (University of Michigan Press, December 21, 2000). Author Nigel Pollard, Ph.D., Professor of Roman History at Oxford University, examined the ethnicity, in detail, of the eastern provinces of Roman soldiers during the first century. After thoroughly reviewing the most recent scholarly writings on the subject, he became convinced that the overwhelming majority of the soldiers who destroyed the Temple were primarily Syrians, Arabs, and Eastern ethnicities. An old reality emerged.

When destroying Jerusalem and the Temple, the soldiers disobeyed their commanders when ordered to quench the Temple fire because their hatred of the Jews overwhelmed their fears of the generals.

https://www.hope-of-israel.org/peopleofprince.html

The people that God so severely punishes were the non-believers in Him and His Son, Jesus Christ. Thus, the preceding verses point directly to

Muslim countries with hate for Israel, the Jewish people, and Christians for centuries. But we must also include those of the world who share that hatred. Whether we like it or not, the fundamental question is, do we live, or not, by the tenets of the Christian religion that claims our most sacred commandment is:

> (Luke 10:27) "'You shall love the LORD your God with all your heart, with all your soul, with all your strength, and with all your mind,' and 'your neighbor as yourself.'"

Alternatively, what happens if we do not? Look around the world – is it getting better or worse? Is there more love between us or more hate? Can you not see why God asked me to author this book? This book is a plea to recognize that we live in the end times. Jesus's return will happen in the lifetime of most of this earth's population. That populace will significantly diminish unless many turn to God and seek the promise of Christ's salvation. The Ottoman Empire of 1917 entered WW1 on the losing side of Germany. As a result, the Empire's dismantling split the Empire into separate countries resulting in its death by fragmentation. Luke's 20:21 prophecy tells us that when armies surround Jerusalem, its desolation is near, alluding to its capture by the Antichrist. Zechariah further describes the battles that will ravish Israel's women as the Antichrist's armies prepare for Armageddon.

## Judgments [Sheep or Goats]

Those who survive the last 3.5 years of the Great Tribulation are the "sheep," with the losers being the "goats." Jesus will decide that sort during the final 3.5 years. Many sheep will survive the Wrath of GOD by renouncing their allegiance to Satan and turning to GOD and Jesus. They will be the flesh and blood portion of the population earning their redemption with random acts of kindness to their fellow man.

Muslim countries surround Israel. It displays the city names within Turkey referenced in the Bible to identify it as the new King of the north [the neo-Ottoman Caliphate]).

(Ezekiel 38) ³I am against you, O Gog, the prince of Rosh, Meshach, and Tubal. ⁵ Persia, Ethiopia, and Libya are with them,

## The END-TIME ATTACK

Reacting to the [2022+] Egyptian attack in Daniel 11, the King of the North, now an early version of the coming neo-Ottoman Caliphate (Syria, Iraq, Iran, Turkey, Egypt), is short of the full-blown ten expected at Armageddon. However, as the early version begins to fight, the Ezekiel 38 battle morphs into the Gog-Magog entity becoming WW111 that starts picking up the necessary countries to become the full-blown ten-nation neo-Ottoman Caliphate Christ will battle at Armageddon. This early version of the beast, Gog-Magog, is just starting to face God incarnate as He returns and lands on Mount Olivet to begin the last 3.5 years of the 7-year tribulation.

But news from the east and north would trouble him. The major countries of those regions would be China, Russia, Pakistan, and India. Although being of the same ilk, the Antichrist's fear must have been that they would infringe on his conquest feeding frenzy. After all, the neo-Ottoman Beast had just planted his palace tents west of the Holy City, between the Mediterranean and the Dead Sea, presumably to govern newly conquered Jerusalem. The implication is that God has already helped him conquer Israel/Jerusalem, as promised in Zech 14:2. When God changes allegiance to serve His people, Gog becomes a temporary winner.

Thus, Antichrist Gog, a younger version of the neo-Ottoman Beast, all being the same, will come to his end, meaning death, with no one to help him. There would be no other allies to support his position, so God ended his life and buried him in the valley of Hamon Gog in what is now the Jordan side of the Dead Sea. This burial on Jordan territory further suggests that Israel claimed that land after defeating Gog.

The magnitude of the battle showed itself by taking *seven months* for the Israelites to bury the dead, after which they would do another search. The searchers then finding any other bones would also mark them for burial. The above facts say that the brutal war left no remaining survivors. It was mainly all the countries west of the Mediterranean. The land, because of the nuclear contamination, would become uninhabitable.

However, God's army, having taken care of the Gog-Magog war by killing the Antichrist, Gog, and burying him in Hamon Gog, began to prepare for the final battle of Armageddon. First, God clarifies that Gog is the Antichrist with His rhetorical question: <u>Are you he of whom I have spoken in former days by My servants the prophets of Israel, who prophesied for years in those days that I would bring you against them?</u> So when God slays the Antichrist, Gog, and physically buries him in Hamongog, the soul arrives "alive" in Hades for its eternal judgment. Next, God tells him what He will do to his army during the last 3.5 years; Every man's sword will be against his brother, and a [20]great earthquake (Rev 6:14) tells <u>"every mountain and island was moved out of its place.</u> Then, a flooding rain will come down on him and his troops, with great hailstones, fire, and brimstone. With the demise of the Antichrist, it would be safe to say: That Gog-Magog was no longer a threat.

The aftermath of the battle left enough weapons for the Israeli citizens living in the cities to collect and use as a fire source ***for seven years*** instead of further decimating the forests in seeking wood.

(Ezekiel 39) [9] "Then those who dwell in the cities of Israel will go out and set on fire and burn the weapons, both the shields and bucklers, the bows and arrows, the [l]javelins and spears; and they will make fires with them ***for seven years.*** [10] They will not take wood from the field nor cut down *any* from the forests because they will make fires with the weapons; they will plunder those who plundered them and pillage those who pillaged them," says the Lord GOD. Thus, they shall "cleanse the land." With the Antichrist leader Gog dead and buried, his presence would be in the bottomless pit.

### Sorting the good from the bad

Good grapes

> (Revelation 14:14 -20) <u>Reaping the Earth's Harvest</u>
> [14]Then I looked, and behold, a white cloud, and on the

cloud sat One like the Son of Man, having on His head a golden crown, and in His hand a sharp sickle. [15]And another angel came out of the temple, crying with a loud voice to Him who sat on the cloud, "Thrust in Your sickle and reap, for the time has come [i]for You to reap, for the harvest of the earth is ripe." [16] So He who sat on the cloud thrust in His sickle on the earth, and the earth was reaped.

After the Rapture, the earth's crop would be its remaining population, scheduled for harvesting as the ripe grapes would be the symbolic 'Born Agains" headed for salvation. Credence to that observation would be the description of the Son of Man, Jesus, wearing a golden crown doing the reaping by following directions of an angel coming out of the Heavenly Temple. All the descriptors in Revelation 14:14-16 show a divine source. Christ had replicated the Rapture: And will take the "ripe grapes," 'born again" to Heaven. These would be akin to the previously raptured: wheat. Contrarily, the winepress for the Grapes of Wrath was outside the Holy City. Remember, these over-ripe grapes represent sinners, and the sour juice is the blood of those undergoing punishment. Furthermore, the descriptive scripture of the final battle places it outside Jerusalem by stating it happens beyond the Holy City walls.

## Grapes of Wrath

(Revelation 14:17-16) Reaping the Grapes of Wrath

[17]Then another angel came out of the temple which is in heaven, he also having a sharp sickle. [18]And another angel came out from the altar, who had power over fire, and he cried with a loud cry to him who had the sharp sickle, saying, "Thrust in your sharp sickle and gather the clusters of the vine of the earth, for her grapes are fully ripe." [19]So the angel thrust his sickle into the earth and gathered the vine of the earth, and threw it into the great winepress of the wrath of God. [20]And the winepress was trampled outside the city, and blood came out of the

winepress, up to the horses' bridles, for one thousand six hundred [k]furlongs. (200 miles).

The Grapes of Wrath's population were the remnant from the <u>sheep</u> and <u>goat</u> sort where the winepress would happen outside of the Holy City and thus link it to Armaggedon at Megiddo, between the Mediterranean and the Gallillian Sea.

> (Revelation 9:16) Sixth Trumpet: The Angels from the Euphrates [13]Then the sixth angel sounded: And I heard a voice from the four horns of the golden altar which is before God, [14]saying to the sixth angel who had the trumpet, "Release the four angels who are bound at the great river Euphrates." [15]So the four angels, who had been prepared for the hour and day and month and year, were released to kill a third of mankind. [16]Now the number of the army of the horsemen was two hundred million; I heard the number of them.

> (Rev 16:16) Sixth Bowl: Euphrates Dried Up [12]Then the sixth angel poured out his bowl on the great river Euphrates, and its water was dried up, so that the way of the kings from the east might be prepared. [13]And I saw three unclean spirits like frogs coming out of the mouth of the dragon, out of the mouth of the beast, and out of the mouth of the false prophet. [14] For they are spirits of demons, performing signs, which go out to the kings of the earth and the whole world, to gather them to the battle of that great day of God Almighty. [15]"Behold, I am coming as a thief. Blessed is he who watches, and keeps his garments, lest he walk naked and they see his shame." [16]And they gathered them together to the place called in Hebrew, Armageddon.

> Joel 2:20, "But I will remove far from you the northern army, and will drive him away into a barren and desolate land, With his face toward the eastern sea

[Sea of Galilee] And his back toward the western sea [Mediterraen]; His stench will come up

Joel2:28 28"And it shall come to pass afterward That I will pour out My Spirit on all flesh; Your sons and your daughters shall prophesy, Your old men shall dream dreams, Your young men shall see visions. 29And also on *My* menservants and on *My* maidservants I will pour out My Spirit in those days.

Joel 2:20 describes God's promise to move His Children far from the northern army and refers to enemy trouble from east of the Euphrates:

Daniel 11:44 But news from the east and the north shall trouble him; therefore he shall go out with great fury to destroy and annihilate many.

This information hints at Megiddo, between the Mediterranean and the Sea of Galilee, as the Armageddon battleground.

Next, God would send His sixth Bowl angel to dry up the Euphrates to allow the east kings access to Israel. Finally, unclean spirits coming from the mouths of the Dragon, the Antichrist, and the False Prophet would invite the spirits to send signs out to the world's kings, calling them to gather for the fantastic Day of battle: Armageddon.

### Where does Armageddon Happen

Christ will thoroughly display His anger in the final battle of Armageddon, on the overwhelming last day of the LORD. The nominations for the encounter location are Megiddo, and the Valley of Jehoshaphat, called out in Joel 3:12-15. However, inferring that the Valley of Jehoshaphat, in Joel 3, will be Armageddon's location is misleading because religious scholars favor the plains of Megiddo; plus, when analyzing Joel 3, the verses lead to a different conclusion.

The Valley of Jehoshaphat runs north and south between the west Temple Mount and the Mount of Olives to the East. It would hardly appear capable of holding all the world's nations, suggesting this inference is not the correct location. Studying the original Hebrew words used in Joel's prophecy may help resolve this misperception.

There are several words for "Valley:" When the Bible refers to deep-sided valleys or gorges such as Kidron or the Valley of Jehoshaphat, it uses the word gay. However, in Joel, the word used is emeq to describe the "Valley" of God's threshing judgments that also means "vale or open country," and, naturally, provides a better fit. Also, the gist of the Hebrew word Jehoshaphat means "Yahweh Has Judged." Furthermore, the prophet Joel also refers to the place of God's judgments as "the Valley of Decision." Thus, the alternative interpretation of the Hebrew word for decision would be "a sharp-edged instrument used for threshing."

I believe God is telling us He will be the sharp-edged threshing tool that brings His winnowing judgment to separate the wheat from the tares when the time is ripe, and the harvest is ready. Armageddon breaks down into three main elements: Arema-gai-dun. When putting the pieces together into a meaningful phrase, these Hebrew words would read "A heap of sheaves in a valley for judgment," reinforcing the idea of a winnowing action during harvest. Replacing the word valley with "open country" leaves A heap of sheaves in the open country ready for God's judgment. Therefore, the Valley of Jehoshaphat is not where the battle will happen. But the words present an account of the punishment that will take place on the wide-open threshing floor of Megiddo, where the world nations would be the sheaves awaiting God's judgment. Still, it would seem that even the broad plains of Megiddo would be inadequate to hold the battling participants of the world, thus suggesting that Megiddo is a metaphor for every place where the nations of the world would await His judgment.

[John Ramsden http://www.biblemagazine.com/magazine/vol-9/issue-1/armag.html] [John Ramsden Armaggedon Where and When Will it Happen?]

Megiddo, where all this action is to take place, is located about 60 miles from Jerusalem in Northern Israel. Therefore, the circumstances seem only fitting that British General Allenby, in 1918, defeated the Turkish Ottoman forces in the same place. He thus killed the "original beast from the sea [comment: "the Ottoman Empire"] by defeating and dismantling it into separate countries. "We saw" The original beast that "was" the former Ottoman Empire, and now "is not" having been killed [separated into individual countries].

It will re-emerge out of the bottomless pit in the form of ten new countries, temporarily forming a new Caliphate to become the "beast that is," the neo-Ottoman Empire, with all its allies, which will fight Christ in the upcoming battle. The battle of Armageddon would be the "return match" against the newly formed Ottoman Empire, still seeking to destroy Israel and Christianity for a Globalized New World Order run by the Antichrist and the False Prophet.

Remember, at this point, only Satan's hardened unbelievers will be the remnant remaining on earth. At the beginning of the last 3.5 years of Wrath, God will send two witnesses to us, clothed in sackcloth, with the power to prophesy over those years. The witnesses would devour the attackers with fire from their mouths if anyone planned to harm them. Moreover, they had the power to control rainfall during their prophetic days, turn waters into blood, and create plagues on the earth as often as they desired. No less than 3.5 days before the Awesome battle, God would allow the Antichrist to kill the two witnesses and leave them dead in the streets. On the day of action, He would then resurrect them in sight of everyone. Those who dwelled on the earth would rejoice and make merry, sending gifts to one another, celebrating their deaths because these two prophets had tormented them. During their resurrection, God would command the two witnesses in a loud voice, "Come up here," causing great fear in those watching them return to life and ascend into heaven. Revelation 11:13 also states that God will resurrect them at the same hour as a great earthquake. Since we know God will revive them on the last day of their 3.5-year assignment, that earthquake has to be the same "never been seen before" on the Awesome Day of the LORD in Revelation16:18.

Knowledge Commentary: An Exposition of the Scriptures, edited by J. F. Walvoord and R. B. Zuck (Wheaton, IL: Victor Books, 1985), states: The seventh trumpet chronologically reaches Christ's return. *Therefore the seventh trumpet introduces and includes the seven bowl judgments of the wrath of God*

## CHRIST RETURNS ON ARMAGEDDON DAY OF THE LORD

The best fit for Christ's coming is Rev 19:11-16, where John describes Christ and His army coming on white horses from an opened heaven to the Armageddon battle.

> (Revelation 19:11-16) [11]Now I saw heaven opened, and behold, a white horse. And He who sat on him was called Faithful and True, and in righteousness, He judges and makes war. [12]His eyes were like a flame of fire, and on His head were many crowns. He had[·] a name written that no one knew except Himself. [13]He was clothed with a robe dipped in blood, [*from treading the grapes of wrath*] and His name is called The Word of God. [14]And the *armies in heaven*, clothed in fine linen, white and clean,[·] followed Him on white horses. [15]Now out of His mouth goes a sharp sword that with it He should strike the nations. And He Himself will rule them with a rod of iron [referring to His future reign]. He Himself treads the winepress of the fierceness and wrath of Almighty God. [16]And He has on His robe and on His thigh a name written:

KING OF KINGS AND LORD OF LORDS.

> [20]Then the Beast [Gog, the Antichrist] was captured and with him the false prophet who worked signs in his presence, by which he deceived those who received the mark of the Beast and those who worshiped his image. These two were cast alive into the lake of fire burning with brimstone. [21]And the rest were killed with the sword which proceeded from the mouth of Him who sat on the horse.

As explained earlier, Trumpet 7 and Bowl 7 coincide and form a "vision" of that last day of God's week announcing Christ's return simultaneous with His Armageddon victory.

The following Trumpet 7 and Bowl 7 scriptures best describe His return:

> (Revelation 11:15) Trumpet 7: [15]then the seventh angel sounded: And there were loud voices in heaven, saying, "The kingdoms of this world have become the kingdoms of our LORD and of His Christ, and He shall reign forever and ever!"

> (Revelation 16:17) Bowl 7: [17]A loud voice came out of the temple of heaven, from the throne, saying, "It is done!"

What better evidence could there be than those words from the Throne of Heaven?

However, we need to be continually aware of some fundamental truths. The Rapture took all of God's "born again" to heaven leaving the remnant as Satan's left behind. Jesus would judge by sorting between the sheep and the goats. He would again change the metaphor to describe Grapes of Wrath as evil to better match the Battle of Armageddon by locating the winepress for the grapes of Wrath outside the walls of the Holy City.

We end up with:

Good = Raptured sheep, Ripe Grapes

Evil = Left Behind, goats, Grapes of Wrath

Thus, we have three different metaphors representing Evil or Good. Constantly referring to the population, using these terms identifies where the events occur during the timeline. It will become clear why this happens as the story continues.

The phrase Day of the LORD, defines itself as one day (Zechariah 14:7) where God avenges Himself, using sudden destruction (1 Thessalonians 5:2) [2]against His adversaries (Jeremiah 46:10). The Tribulation implies many such days occur of sequential punishments throughout Daniel's seven years.

> (Joel 2:31) It tells us that: [31]the sun shall be turned into darkness and the moon into blood before the coming of the great and fantastic day of the LORD.

Joel suggests that the aforementioned celestial display is massively destructive and will happen before the implied, far worse, <u>awesome day of the LORD.</u> These days, collectively, we could combine giving an <u>epochal gist</u> to the Tribulation as comprised of multiple, sequential <u>Days of the LORD,</u> leaving us to wonder about the fantastic day yet to come: what can be worse, and when will it happen?

Since the Bible likens the Tribulation to pregnancy with birth pains that grow exponentially worse until delivery, the most severe agony occurs at birth: i.e., the last day of the 6000-year God's week. So, what will make this single day so vastly different?

<u>This last fantastic Day of the LORD, when Christ returns,</u> is a moment when God's wrath blends into a unique, terrible day of punishment, the likes of which humanity has never seen. The Gog-Magog war will work its way through the Western Islamic countries between the shores of the Dead Sea and the Mediterranian and then cross the Euphrates where all the remnant Islamic nations will face Christ in the last battle: Armageddon. It would stop just short of destroying humanity. The war between Christ and the Antichrist, leading his army of all the world's nations, would continue throughout the last 3.5 years culminating on the final day: Armageddon. With Nibiru close, causing mountains and islands to disappear, it would produce a massive earthquake, creating large tsunamis and hurricane winds. Nibiru's proximity also would temporarily knock the earth out of its orbit. Billions will die in this single day that prophesies two-thirds of the population or more will perish, leaving 2.4 billion, or even less, to persevere and remain alive to enter Christ's millennial kingdom. At best, after the final battle, God will put His Son in charge of the promised thousand years of peace and Godly rule while condemning Satan to the bottomless pit with the Antichrist and the False Prophet into the Lake of fire. Jesus will <u>embrace His triumphant victory</u> at Armageddon and show He is ready to begin His millennial reign in Jerusalem.

## THE END OF CHRIST RETURNS

www.ingramcontent.com/pod-product-compliance
Lightning Source LLC
Chambersburg PA
CBHW051518120626

46551CB00012B/974

* 9 7 9 8 9 8 6 4 2 8 3 0 7 *